D0477389

Royalties to the National Playing Fields Association

MUSICAL BUMPS

Dudley Moore

Illustrated by John Jensen

Robson Books

First published in Great Britain in 1986 by Robson Books Ltd.,
Bolsover House,   5-6 Clipstone Street,   London W1P 7EB.

copyright ©1986 Dudley Moore
Illustrations copyright © 1986 John Jensen

British Library Cataloguing in Publication Data

Moore, Dudley
   Musical bumps-
   1. Music—Anecdotes, facetial, satire, etc.
   I. Title
   780   ML65

ISBN 0-86051-401-3

Typesetting and origination by:
Grainger Photosetting Ltd., Southend-on-Sea, Essex

Printed by St Edmundsbury Press Ltd.,
Bury St Edmunds, Suffolk.

Contents

Introduction

I received my first musical bump at a very tender age when I was summarily informed that I was too small to carry the cross at the head of the church choir. Sometimes it seems as if, in its darker moments, my career has been a series of minor prangs ever since.

When the time came for me to apply for a place at one of the principal London music schools my music teacher was adamant that I should put down the Royal College or the Royal Academy as my first choice, having little faith in the Guildhall School of Music, for some reason. However, my mother, realizing that it was a shorter Tube journey to the Guildhall from our home in Dagenham, by about two stops, pointed me in that direction. So my music teacher's delight at my winning a junior exhibition was considerably diluted when she heard which school had awarded it to me.

A knock of a rather different sort was delivered when the time came for me to take my next step up the musical ladder and enter for an organ scholarship at Magdalen (beware: the name of this Oxford college is pronounced 'maudlin'!). At that stage in the Sixth Form most people get into the habit of delivering amazingly cosmic but certainly heartfelt utterances and I was no exception. Discussing the forthcoming scholarship exam with a friend one day I announced, 'You know it could make my life if I get it, or it could ruin it if I don't.' The headmaster happened to be passing by and, hearing this, took me to one side and said coolly, 'Don't get affected.'

When I got to Oxford it was my tutor who was sometimes forced to take a slightly jaundiced view of my attitude, especially when we tackled the duller parts of the syllabus. I was rather depressed when he once characterized me as a miniaturist, thinking for a moment that he was referring to my height and the persistence with which I clung to it. Of course a moment's thought led me to the truth, that presenting six bars of a Palestrina exercise was just not enough for the tutorial and he was basically saying, 'Pull your socks up or you'll be out on the streets like everybody else.'

Came my finals, I went in to the exams to sit a paper on the Purcell Trio Sonatas, our special subject if you chose the Baroque period, as I had done. These had somehow escaped my attention until a week before the paper, and looking down it my eyes settled on the question that anyone in their right mind would ask, and anyone who hadn't studied them would dread, namely: 'Enumerate and describe the polyphonic devices used by Purcell in his Trio Sonatas.' I set off by suggesting that concentrating on petty details like these was really rather *infra dig.* and then waffled on for a few pages. It was so curious. I was terribly afraid of failing and yet a lemming-like quality that seemed to follow me everywhere put me into awful predicaments like this.

Still I managed to scrape through, started earning a living at the keyboard and in the fullness of time found myself part of *Beyond the Fringe*, where I met Jonathan Miller (along with Alan Bennett and Peter Cook) who dubbed me 'a grubby cherub' and dismissed music, at least in those days, as 'orange juice for the ears' – great boosts for the ego. The programme (price one shilling) I've preserved from the London production reveals that this revue, which was on Broadway from 1962 to 1964, was 'originally conceived and produced for the Edinburgh Festival by John Bassett', had its first performance on Wednesday 10 May 1061, and that I composed or arranged all the music.

It was during the run of *Beyond the Fringe*, when we had a week off and I was going to Portofino, that I met Sir John Gielgud at the airport. He told me that I should say hello to Lili Palmer, who was living out there, and I said that I'd love to, feeling slightly apprehensive at the idea of presenting myself at a famous actress's house for no reason at all. However, he gave me a note of introduction and sent me on my way. Once we were safely airborne, I opened the envelope and read, 'Darling Lili, this is to introduce the young pianist from *Beyond the Fringe*, Stanley Moon.'! I never did have the nerve to present myself to Miss Palmer. And so it's gone on.

Looking on the brighter side, though, ricocheting about the musical world has at least enabled me to have a taste of everything from choral singing to cabaret, from madrigals to movie composition and from locations as varied as a bar in Greenwich Village (where I eked out what passed for a Bohemian existence) and Carnegie Hall (where I appeared opulently and rather self-consciously attired in white tie and tails). Together, these experiences have taught me not to take the musical world (as opposed to the music itself) too seriously – as I hope this collection of musical bits and pieces shows.

In the pages that follow you'll find an assortment of scraps and odds and ends from musical history which I have found amusing and interesting. If some of the great names of musical history are shown in a less august light than is usually their lot, I hope these jottings and peeps behind the scene add a further depth and dimension to their characters as they're generally portrayed.

Similarly if in some of the anecdotes and quotations the milk of human kindness has curdled more than a trifle (sorry) it simply shows the vicarious delight I've taken in picking out a few musical bumps suffered by others!

Wait a Minim!

Even from an early age I've been fascinated by the way that music is made whether in listening to our old gramophone or watching an intricate counterpoint as it works its way through a score.

This wasn't always to the advantage of my own musical development. There was a time (which actually lasted for many years) when I was obsessed with the technical side of music – agonizing about the physical side of my piano-playing, sometimes to the exclusion of listening to what I was playing, the importance of which has only dawned on me fully comparatively late in my musical career.

When I was younger I was more catholic in my range of instruments. Brief flirtations with an old piece of bakelite, which I think called itself a Tipperary flute (the only wind instrument I ever attempted) and the cello (with which I formed one sixth of an ensemble at a school Speech Day as we screeched our way through an excruciating perform-ance of 'Frère Jacques' while the audience were barely able to contain their laughter) were soon abandoned as I concentrated on the violin and the piano, which led later to the organ.

Drawn towards the piano in the living-room at home, I was soon playing it endlessly, experiencing the thrill of early discoveries like the sequence in classical harmony which is found in so many popular songs in some way or other. I remember discovering this and playing it endlessly, mesmerized by the wonderfully comforting sound it produced.

It seems right then to kick off with a look at what you might term the more technical side of music making, taking perhaps a rather oblique glance at musical instruments, the ways in which they are played, a little musical terminology and the means by which most of us 'make music' – recorded music.

> *Sir Thomas Beecham, to an orchestra: 'Forget about bars. Look at the phrases, please. Remember that bars are only the boxes in which the music is packed.'*

Tunnel Vision

Sir Isaac Newton, who was modest enough about his own scientific endeavours – describing them as being like a child wandering along a seashore and picking up coloured pebbles here and there – didn't show any greater enthusiasm for the achievements of his great contemporaries in other fields. On hearing Handel playing the harpsichord, all that Newton could think of saying afterwards was that he had a wonderful elasticity in his fingers.

Mind you, I can sympathize with Newton in a way. His might well have been a coldly scientific observation that remained unmoved by the music and totally missed the point of Handel's performance, but, having no variation in tone, the harpsichord is not the most expressive instrument in the world and it does require considerable technical ability to draw the full spirit of a piece from it.

Edison's Ten Predictions for Future Uses of His Phonograph

The phonograph that Edison invented in 1877 may have had modest beginnings (the first message recorded was 'Halloo' and the contents of the first 'record' was 'Mary had a little lamb') but the great inventor foresaw huge possibilities for his creation, which he listed the year after patenting his brainchild.

1 Letter writing through dictaphones
2 Talking books for the blind
3 Teaching elocution
4 Playing recorded music
5 Recording voices for a family record
6 Providing the apparatus for toys, like talking dolls
7 Speaking clocks
8 Recording the voices of famous personalities
9 Audio educational aid
10 Telephone answering service

Musical Accountability — Or the Industrial Engineer's Report on a Symphony Played at a Promenade Concert

1   It was noted that for considerable periods the four players employed in the oboe section were inactive. It is advised that work should be spread evenly throughout the whole orchestra, thereby eliminating wasteful peaks and troughs of activity.

2   It was also noted that the twelve players assigned to playing the violin were playing identical notes; this also suggests an intolerable level of duplication. Cuts in personnel could be easily implemented in this area. In the event of an increased volume being required, it is advised that electronic amplification equipment be employed.

3   There was a great deal of attention paid to the playing of demi-semiquavers (thirty-second notes); this too appears to be an unnecessary refinement. The recommendation is that all notes should be rounded up to the nearest semi-quaver (sixteenth note). This would be a cost-effective measure by providing an opening for employing trainees and lower-grade operatives in place of the skilled staff currently undertaking this work.

4   There was also considerable repetition of a number of musical passages, leading to the conclusion that scores could be drastically pruned. Little useful purpose would seem to be served by the woodwind repeating a passage that has already been handled, for example, by the string section. The elimination of redundant passages such as these would lead, it is estimated, to a significant reduction of the playing time from 120 minutes (2 hours) to 20 minutes ($\frac{1}{3}$ hour), so removing the need for an intermission, and the contingent provision of refreshment facilities and staff.

5 While agreeing with these conclusions in outline, the conductor has expressed the opinion that they might lead, in some degree, to a decline in audience attendance. If box office returns indicate this to be the case, it would seem sensible to arrange for sections of the concert hall to be closed completely, with resulting savings in overheads like heating and lighting. In the final event of audiences falling off still further, the Royal Albert Hall could be abandoned completely and the concerts transferred to premises better suited to their new conditions.

Popular Musical Fallacies
from the Age of Reason

In 1767 Jean-Jacques Rousseau published his *Dictionnaire de Musique*, Mozart was eleven years old, and it might be fair to expect that a sensible and reasoned approach to music, and all the other civilized arts, coloured the age. However, 1767 also saw the publication of a series of essays that show this was far from being the case. In his work *A New Catalogue of Vulgar Errors* Stephen Fovargue listed thirty-six popular fallacies he could pinpoint in his day, a surprising number of which had to do with the understanding and playing of music.

Here I have listed the 'errors' that Fovargue picked on, to show how even in the most apparently enlightened age some pretty odd notions about one of its most flourishing art forms could exist.

That the tone of a violin is to be brought out, by laying on like a blacksmith.

That the violin is a wanton instrument, and not proper for psalms; and that the organ is not proper for country-dances, and brisk airs.

That the Organ and Harpsichord are the two principal instruments, and that other instruments are inferior to them in a concert.

That every key in music ought to have a different effect or sound.

That a piece of music which has flats set before it, is in a flat key on that account, and vice versa with sharps.

That the musical composition of this present age is inferior to that of the last.

That the hearing of musical performances is apt to soften men too much, and by that means to give them an effeminate manner.

That the Italian operas consist of effeminate musick.

I Love a Piano

When Irving Berlin used this as the title of a popular song in 1915, he was echoing the thoughts of many. George Bernard Shaw said, 'The pianoforte is the most important of all musical instruments: its invention was to music what the invention of printing was to poetry.'

Perhaps he had heard the Italian proverb 'He who plays the piano keeps sane.' A charming thought, but scarcely accurate when you remember the large number of pianists – from Robert Schumann to Scott Joplin – who have died in a lunatic asylum. Another anonymous proverb is probably nearer the mark, 'Old piano players never die, they simply fake away!'

Sir Thomas Beecham was renowned for his love of the piano, which was only equalled by his hatred of the harpsichord, the sound of which he described as being like, 'two skeletons copulating on a galvanized tin roof.' (That's really a bit unfair considering what a hard instrument the harpsichord is to play.)

In the hands of a master, however, the piano can make an audience happier than anything else in the world. Such a man is Liberace, who explains, 'My whole trick is to keep the tune well out in front. If I play Tchaikovsky I play his melodies and skip his spiritual struggles. Naturally I condense. I have to know just how many notes my audience will stand for. If there's time left over I fill in with a lot of runs up and down the keyboard.'

When asked why the keys of his piano were so yellow, Victor Borge replied that it wasn't so much that the piano was old as that 'the elephant smoked too much...'

(The keys on my piano at home were very yellow too and because the poor thing had been so hammered earlier in its existence I'll always associate yellow with loudness.)

As far back as the sixteenth century it was decided that the keyboard was a form of musical instrument that a woman could play decorously, which is why the name 'virginals' was given to early members of the harpsichord family. Gradually instruments like the flute were added to the female repertoire, although the Victorians drew the line at the cello, which they considered to be wholly indecent. The pressure to allow women to play it was such, however, that a compromise was eventually reached in the form of the side-saddle cello!

The tune of the Westminster chimes is probably the most widely played tune in the world. Clocks that play part of the tune every quarter of an hour chime it 35,040 times a year (35,136 times in a leap year), and in the course of the average lifetime anyone growing up in a house with such a clock will hear the tune over a million times.

The Music Lovers

One man's music is another man's noise pollution, as the *Guardian* newspaper reported recently when a dispute arose in Cambridge between two music lovers of a very different kind.

Dr George Guest, who is a university organist and director of the much acclaimed St John's College choir, complained to the city council about busker Chris Tabecki's melodeon playing.

Mr Tabecki was a great favourite with the market traders of Cambridge, but his repertoire didn't go down at all well with Dr Guest, who called in the environmental health officer in his bid to rid himself of the noise nuisance. After exchanges of opinion, a solution to the discord was found. Mr Tabecki will only play his melodeon on Saturdays when Dr Guest is not in his rooms at St John's.

When I was a music student I used to play jazz on the college organ now and again, and I also used it for recording music I'd written for plays: the chapel had a built-in echo that made it an ideal recording studio. Working on the music for a sea battle one day I'd recorded sound effects of timber crashing from sound-effects records, which approximated to ships colliding at sea. On the other side of the tape I then recorded some fanfares I'd written to be played during the battle while another scene was going on on stage. By a technical quirk that I never understood the two pieces bled together through the tape and, mixed by some unseen hand, proved to very effective. Sessions like that used to land me in much the same position as Mr Tabecki with the fellows of my college.

\# * Anyone for noughts & crosses?

My bowels shall sound like a harp.

Isaiah 16:11

To Be Read Aloud

A tutor who tooted a flute
Tried to teach two young tutors to toot;
Said the two to the tutor:
'Is it harder to toot, or
To tutor two tutors to toot?'

Anon.

Organized!

The very first organ ever built was invented by a Greek engineer called Ktesibios, who lived in Alexandria, Egypt, in the third century BC. We know this because his organ was one of the most amazing inventions of his day. Pliny the Elder was so excited by it that he called it one of the wonders of the world. Because it used water in its pipes to help stabilize the air pressure it was called *hydraulis* – which greatly confused medieval musicians when, centuries later, they tried to recreate it. Figuring that it must have been run by a water mill or even steam, because of its name, they had a terrible time trying to copy it!

Ancient inventions with unfamiliar names can be traced directly through the ages to modern instruments. Do you have any idea what the modern descendant of the shawm is, for example? Or the gittern? (Shawm = oboe; gittern = guitar.)

Definitions like this remind me of a sketch I did with Peter Cook that went along the lines of a conversation about sex that included the exchange:

Pete: I looked up the word 'bastard' the other day. It's the worst, most disgusting word in the English language, 'bastard'. It said in the dictionary it's 'A child born out of wedlock.'
Dud: What's a 'wedlock' Pete?
Pete: I think it's a cross between a steam engine and a padlock.

The Devil's Consort

When Ambrose Bierce disappeared in 1913 during the Mexican Civil War, I think there might have been just a few musicians who felt that he'd met up with the avenging god of music, against whom Bierce had composed some of the sharpest entries in his writings that later became *The Devil's Dictionary*. George Bernard Shaw had written in *Man and Superman* that 'music is the brandy of the damned' and in Bierce's writing the 'devil' had a lot to say about it, especially with respect to the instruments that create it. These are some of my favourite Bierce definitions:

Accordion   An instrument in harmony with the sentiments of an assassin

Bassoon   A brazen instrument into which a fool blows out his brains

Clarinet   An instrument of torture operated by a person with cotton in his ears. There are two instruments that are worse than a clarinet – two clarinets

Cremona   A high-priced kind of violin made in Connecticut. A genuine Connecticut Cremona is supposed to be mentioned in the following lines of Omar Khayyam:

> Hey, diddle, diddle!
> The cat got the fiddle,
> The cow jumped over the moon,
> But the little dog stayed
> To hear the thing played,
> And died of the very first tune.

Fiddle   An instrument to tickle human ears by the friction of a horse's tail on the entrails of a cat.

Flute A variously perforated hollow stick intended for the punishment of sin, the minister of retribution being commonly a young man with straw coloured eyes and lean hair.

Jew's harp An unmusical instrument, played by holding it fast with the teeth and trying to brush it away with the finger.

Lyre An ancient instrument of torture. The word is now used in a figurative sense to denote the poetic faculty, as in the following fiery lines of the great poet, Ella Wheeler Wilcox:

I sit astride Parnassus with my lyre
And pick with care the disobedient wire.
The stupid shepherd lolling on his crook
With deaf attention scarcely deigns a look.

I bide my time, and it shall come at length,
When, with Titan's energy and strength,
I'll grab a fistful of strings, and O,
The world shall suffer when I let them go!

Piano A parlour utensil for subduing the impertinent visitor. It is operated by depressing the keys of the machine and the spirits of the audience.

To enable an orchestra to tune up, Sir Thomas Beecham asked the principal oboist for an 'A'. Noting that the player had a rather wide vibrato, Beecham looked around the orchestra and said, 'Gentlemen, take your pick.'

In November 1974 a New York 'musician' recorded a disc ideally suited to anyone who has never found full satisfaction with any form of music yet recorded. In his 'Auditory Memory', Jerry Cammarate offers his listeners 52 minutes, 10 seconds of pure, uninterrupted silence. Not that he was alone in appreciating the commercial possibilities of peace and quiet. Twenty-one years earlier CBS had entered the entertainment market with a novel recording called 'Three Minutes of Silence', which offered the long-suffering customers of juke-box-afflicted haunts just that.

The Real Musical Bump!

The Earl of Harewood – until recently the head of English National Opera – is not a noted member of the criminal fraternity. He did, however, have a brush with the law in 1978, when he backed his car into another which was fitted with a loud security alarm.

In court, charged with leaving the scene of an accident, Lord Harewood's defence was that the sound of the alarm was like that of the clarinet in the Mozart Serenade to which he was listening on the car radio. Whether this says more about the quality of the clarinet playing, the Earl's musical ear, or the wonderful timbre of security alarms these days is not recorded. In any event, the case was dismissed!

Musical Numbers

During his lifetime Joseph Schillinger became a popular and influential composer. Born in Russia, he had works commissioned to celebrate the revolution of 1917, in accordance with his post as composer for the State Academic Theatre of Drama in Leningrad and later dean of the State Academy of Music. In 1930 he emigrated to the USA, where he took up teaching posts in New York.

Some years after his arrival he gave a public performance of a recent composition and asked his audience which composer it reminded them of. Some suggested Mozart; others Bach, Beethoven, Brahms or Debussy. They were reasonable guesses, but it would have taken a fluke for anyone to hit on Schillinger's actual source, which had in fact been the stock-market quotations from the financial pages of his newspaper. In accordance with the remarkable theory he had evolved, Schillinger had plotted these meticulously on a sheet of graph paper and then given each a proportional musical value. The result was the Mozart/Bach/Beethoven/Brahms/Debussy piano sonata that his listeners had just been enjoying.

This technique was no wild flight of fancy, however. Schillinger had been working systematically for several years on his mathematical arrangements, based on a careful study of the similar propensities he had noted in the works of great composers, such as those with which his own composition had been likened. 'My belief is', he once wrote, 'that because music has been created by intuitive or trial-and-error methods and there has never been any scientific investigation of the resources, there is more new unexploited material in forms in music than in any other field subjected to scientific investigation.' Following this principle he went on to show that, just as music could be composed by following formulae, the music of the great composers could similarly be plotted on graphs, where discernible mathematical patterns became evident. During his teaching years in New York, Schillinger extended this theory beyond music and applied it to the investigation of other art forms: graphic art, sculpture, literature, cinema and even speech.

It was as a musician that he won his greatest public following, though. His works were performed frequently by leading orchestras both in America and Europe, while famous musicians like Benny Goodman, Tommy Dorsey, Glenn Miller, Oscar Levant, and George Gershwin received tuition from him. Gershwin studied with him three times a week for four and a half years, during which time he composed *Porgy and Bess*, while Glenn Miller is said to have written 'Moonlight Serenade' as an exercise set him by Schillinger.

The jazz saxophonist, Sonny Rollins, once explained why he always practised with a lighted candle in the room. By playing as close as he could to the candle's flame, he said, he was able to judge his embouchure. If the flame flickered, he knew that air must be escaping from round the reed and his lips weren't tight enough around it.

'Who was that oboe I saw you with last night?'
'That was no oboe, that was my fife!'

The Italian term 'Bel Canto' means literally 'Beautiful Song', and is applied to a certain kind of operatic singing. Many music teachers and critics will tell you that the most appropriate English translation of this is 'Can Belto'!

Ut, Re, Mi, Fa, Sol, La

It's just as well for Richard Rodgers and Oscar Hammerstein that a couple of changes were made to the medieval hexachord from which our *doh, re, mi, fah, sol, la, ti* system originated – imagine the problems that would have arisen trying to write 'Doe a deer' in *The Sound of Music* if the first note was still referred to as 'Ut'?

These minor limitations aside, the original hexachord was a masterpiece of ingenuity and good luck, stumbled on by an eleventh-century monk named Guido d'Arezzo. He came up with the idea that singers could learn a new melody by relating its notes to the pitches of certain syllables associated with a well-known tune, and luck was with him when he came across the very tune he needed in a Latin hymn composed four hundred years earlier. This was one sung by choirboys to St John the Baptist, appropriately seeking the saint's protection against the risks of their going hoarse. Listening to this, Guido noticed that the pitches on which the first syllables of the first six lines were sung happened to be one note higher than the previous one. By applying these syllables and their pitches to the notes of any melody, Guido concluded that a singer could sing that new melody without having previously heard it. Singers have been thanking him for that ever since.

The ascending six-note scale that Guido discovered developed from the ancient hymn in this way:

C *Ut* queant laxis
D *Re*sonare fibris
E *Mi*ra gestorum
F *Fa*muli tuorum
G *Sol*ve polluti
A *La*bii reatum
Sancte Johannes

Apart from the change of *Ut* to *Doh* and the addition of *Ti* for the seventh degree of the scale, these syllables have remained unaltered since Guido hit on their significance almost a thousand years ago.

Back in the last century there was a vogue for very rapid instrument playing which led to some curious and not very pleasing competitions and wagers. Someone who took part in one of the most celebrated of these was a certain Mr Scarborough, organist of Spalding in Lincolnshire. He made a bet that he could strike one million notes on a piano in the space of twelve hours. The challenge was accepted and, taking a spread of three octaves, ascending and descending different scales, he proceeded to strike the notes as follows:

> *109,296 notes in his first hour*
> *125,928 notes in his second hour*
> *121,176 notes in his third hour*
> *121,176 notes in his fourth hour*
> *125,136 notes in his fifth hour*
> *125,136 notes in his sixth hour*
> *127,512 notes in his seventh hour*
> *127,512 notes in his eighth hour*
> *47,520 notes in his final twenty minutes*

In a little over eight hours he managed to strike a total of 1,030,392 notes, which, added to the breaks that he allowed himself, ran to just under the agreed twelve hour period. In my anxiety as a child to perfect my technique that's just the sort of exercise that would have brought me to my knees.

Singing Stars

Far back in the ancient world, the belief in the 'music of the spheres' was developed, to be carried down through literature and folklore into the great masterpieces of English writing. In the Book of Job, chapter 38, verse 7, there's a reference to the harmonies believed to originate from the movement of the stars through space, 'When the morning stars sang together, and all the sons of God shouted for joy.'

To the ancient Greeks the singing stars were reduced to the seven 'wandering stars', the five primary planets: Mercury, Venus, Mars, Jupiter and Saturn, and the Sun and the Moon. In their belief, each was tuned to a note in the harmonic scale and sounded this as it moved through the heavens.

Shakespeare expressed the idea in *The Merchant of Venice* when he gave Lorenzo the lines:

> There's not the smallest orb which thou behold'st
> But in his motion like an angel sings,
> Still quiring to the young-eyed cherubins

So did Milton in the *Ode on the Nativity:*

> Ring out, ye crystal spheres,
> Once bless our human ears,
> (If ye have power to touch our senses so)
> And let your silver chime
> Move in melodious time;
> And let the bass of heaven's deep organ blow;
> And with your ninefold harmony
> Make up full concert to the angelic symphony.

While Wordsworth wrote in *The Triad:*

> And every motion of his starry train
> Seems governed by a strain
> Of music, audible to him alone.

Never lend your wife or your violin – both are sure to come back damaged.

Henri Vieuxtemps.

English As She Is Writ

The Australian-born composer, Percy Grainger, made a determined, some would say idiosyncratic stand, on behalf of Anglo-Saxon, or at least English-based attitudes, in both his life and work. This was most apparent in his use of the English language, a use he was determined should be free of foreign influence. Now, given that music was his chosen profession, doing away with Italian, French, Latin and Greek-based words and phrases required some ingenuity, but Grainger managed, though not always to the improvement of his mother tongue.

In marking his musical scores in particular, he adopted a curious selection of words which conformed to his idea of 'Blue-eyed English', of which these are some of the more entertaining:

appasionato	soul-stirring
ben marcato	well to the fore
chamber music	room music
crescendo molto	louden hugely
duo	twosome
espressivo e legato	feelingly and clingingly
finale	end-piece
intermezzo	between-piece
legato	smoothly
poco meno mosso	very slightly slower
rallentando	slow off
solo	to the fore
sonore	rich
sostenuto	lingeringly
staccato ma pesante	short and heavy

Percy Grainger played on one of the most memorable recordings I've ever heard. This was the Grieg Piano Concerto, which he recorded near the end of his life. Grainger was great friends with Grieg and his feeling for the music makes this recording one that Benjamin Britten regarded as being among the greatest romantic interpretations of any work he'd ever heard.

I wasn't sure what to expect when I first heard it. There was Grainger, thinking that he might pop off at any minute, playing for all he was worth and hitting so many wrong notes it was hard to believe – yet producing a sound so thrilling that it made my hair stand on end. It still has that effect on me, wrong notes and all.

There is one great similarity between music and cricket – there are slow movements in both.

Neville Cardus

Umo

Some years ago I was turning out some old rubbish in the attic when I discovered what looked like a very old musical instrument. It looked promising, but try as I might I couldn't find out how to play it and eventually it got lost again.

Now I think I know what it was – a UMO. UMO stands for Unidentified Musical Object – or instrument, as the case may be – and there may be quite a few of them about.

Two of the most interesting and mysterious UMOs are the doucaine and the cornamuse. The doucaine was mentioned widely in medieval European literature over a period of several hundred years. The cornamuse was a Renaissance instrument. Both of them apparently had a soft, melodious sound and were very easy on the ear. A number of pieces were written for them. Despite that, no one really knows what either of them were or what they looked like.

The doucaine was possible an early type of flute or recorder. The cornamuse might have been a reed instrument, a sort of basic clarinet. So next time you're poking about at a jumble sale or in the loft and you come across a peculiar piece of piping or an odd instrument treat it with respect. It could, for all you know, be a UMO!

Bring on the Animals

I remember once appearing on television as part of the panel on a musical quiz show in which I started becoming faintly embarrassed at the number of questions I couldn't answer. They played me a piece of music which I knew perfectly well because I'd played it endlessly myself, but its name completely escaped me and I had to be told it was the little G minor fugue by Bach. For my next question they asked me to identify a quartet by Haydn and gave me the absurdly obvious clue like, 'You may find this a little sharp on the ear.' I saw myself slipping down the hill into oblivion and said rather flippantly, 'It must be from the razor quartet.' Apparently it was, and I've taken more than a passing interest in musical nicknames ever since.

For example there are the animals. Animals have given their names to dozens of popular nicknames by which a broad range of musical compositions have become known. Here is a selection of twenty. Try covering the right-hand column to see how many you can identify.

Bear Symphony	Symphony no.82 in C (Haydn)
Bee's Wedding	Song without Words in C, op.67, no.4 (Mendelssohn)
Bird Quartet	String quartet no.39, op.33, no.5 (Haydn)
Butterfly Study	Etude in G flat, op.25, no.9 (Chopin)
Cat's Fugue	Sonata in G minor (Scarlatti)
Cuckoo Concerto	Concerto in A minor (Vivaldi)
Cuckoo Sonata	Sonata op.79 in G (Beethoven)
Death of a Wombat	Impressions for Orchestra (Englis)
Dog Waltz	Waltz no.6 in D flat, op.64, no.1 (Chopin)
Donkey Quartet	String quartet op.76, no.2 in D (Haydn)
Flight of the Bumble Bee	*Tsar Sultan* (opera) Act 3 (Rimsky-Korsakov)
Frog Quartet	String quartet no.49 in D, op.50, no.6 (Haydn)
Goldfinch Concerto	6 concerti, op.10, no.3 in G (Vivaldi)

Hen Symphony	Symphony no.12 (Haydn)
Lark Quartet	String quartet no.67, op.64-5 (Haydn)
Nightingale Concerto	Concerto in G minor for violin and orchestra (Perkins)
Sheep May Safely Graze	Cantata no.208 (Bach)
Tadpoles	Symphony no.8 in B flat major (A. Williams)
Trout Quintet	Piano quintet in A (Schubert)
Wasps	Aristophonic suite (Vaughan Williams)

In the early days of sound recording there were all kinds of problems in recording live performances. It's bad enough in these days of refined sound balance and microphones; you only have to remind an audience that this is a live recording and they turn from a perfectly normal, quiet bunch of people into a choking, sneezing, crisp-eating mass. Can you imagine what it was like in the early decades of this century? One early recording of a Cesar Franck symphony in a cathedral picked up a classic problem. When the engineers played back their wax discs on which the performance was recorded they found that all their hard work had been for nothing. For there, at the end of the first movement, perfectly clear and quite ineradicable, came the sound of a woman's voice asking the question: 'Tell me, dear, where do you buy your stockings?' Just because of her thoughtless remark the entire set of records had to be scrapped, and for years the work was known in recording circles as 'the stockings symphony'!

Sir Arthur Sullivan had foreseen problems when he first heard a phonograph played, and wrote to Thomas Edison:

Dear Mr Edison,
For myself, I can only say that I am astonished and somewhat terrified at the result of this evening's experiment. Astonished at the wonderful form you have developed and terrified at the thought that so much hideous and bad music will be put on records for ever.

Elgar – Abbey Road

Thirty-eight years before the Beatles' album *Abbey Road* entered the British hit parade to climb to number one and stay in the charts for seventy-six weeks, Sir Edward Elgar had also visited the famous recording studios – to open them, in November 1931. These were the first studios built and designed in Britain for the sole purpose of recording.

Haydn Seek

The Haydn I'm concerned with here isn't Joseph, but his younger and lesser known brother Michael. It isn't even Michael himself that I want to dwell on, but the extraordinary and quite innocent confusion that one of his works, the 'Flute Concerto in D major', caused in recording circles – at least you might have thought it was one work, but as you'll see, even that wasn't quite as straightforward as you'd imagine.

The problem arose from two independent recordings of the Haydn work, 'Flute Concerto in D major'. One was made in America in the 1950s, the second followed ten years later and on the other side of the Atlantic in Hungary. By a bizarre quirk of fate, both companies chose to give their recording the same classification number, 11530. If that didn't cause enough confusion, it transpired that they had actually recorded two *different* flute concertos in D major written by Michael Haydn.

So two different works by the same composer, were the subject of two different recordings, given the same record number – not a situation that is likely to make the younger Haydn's music any more accessible to, or better known by, the record listening public.

If I were to begin life again, I would devote it to music. It is the only cheap and unpunished rapture on earth.

Sydney Smith

RPM

The year I was born (1935) the Talking Books for the Blind produced records that revolved at 24rpm. These were just some of the specialist discs that have come and gone in the history of recorded music, offering a wide range of speeds that extend from 16²/₃rpm right up to 120rpm.

When I first listened to records they were invariably 78s, which had been going strong for almost forty years. One of the earliest records I remember hearing was Ernest Lough's 'Oh for the wings of a dove', which my parents loved playing, and which must have started my love of English choral music. As a child I used to keep looking down the speaker cover to see if I could see the choir: I was convinced they were in there somewhere. I may not have understood much about the workings of the gramophone but I was captivated by what it could do with those big flat discs.

The first 33¹/₃rpm discs were nine years older than me, although the long playing 33¹/₃ one didn't appear until I was fifteen, to be followed a year later by that other mainstay of the present-day record industry, the 45rpm 7-inch disc. Together these two speeds (and sizes) have dominated the post-war music scene. EPs have come and gone, and the dear old 78s had virtually disappeared by the 1960s.

Just to show that technology isn't standing still, though, there's been a development in recent years to produce 12-inch records that play at 45rpm, some of which provide not far short of half an hour's playing. The extra speed enhances the quality of the sound, but manages to cause confusion along the way, since most of us are so conditioned now to playing 12-inch LPs at 33¹/₃ rpm, that it takes one unsettling lowering of the needle, its immediate raising and the change of the speed knob, to remind us that seeing is not necessarily believing when it comes to listening – if you see what I mean.

The oboe is an ill wind that nobody blows good.

Anon.

Dag Days

I was born in Dagenham, but despite that I'd be the first to admit that it's not the kind of place you'd normally think of as deserving three stars on a musical map. Don't dismiss Dagenham, however, for it has two claims to musical fame. According to whom you talk to (and there are still a few of them about), I'm one; the other is the Dagenham Girl Pipers, one of the most unlikely and most impressive musical phenomena you're ever likely to come across. They had amazing connotations for me as a young boy; I was always hoping I'd bump into one of them on the 148 bus. In fact you could say that Dagenham is the greatest stronghold of the Scotish bagpipes and the kilt south of the border; it certainly was for me. Quite why anyone would want to found a group of girl bagpipers in Dagenham in 1932 I don't know, but they did, and they're still going strong. What's more, they are so good at what they do that they've won over the hearts of many a Scottish audience with their talent. And they also have the distinction of having the first woman Pipe Major in the world. Quite what Jerome K. Jerome would have made of it all I don't know, particularly in the early days of the DGPs. For, as he says in *Three Men in a Boat*, 'There is, it must be confessed, something very sad about the early efforts of an amateur in bagpipes.'

When I was young, my favourite records were always HMV ones. Not, I hasten to add, always because of their content, but because of the record label itself, which featured that little white dog listening to the gramophone. The story behind the record label makes interesting reading. The dog was called Nipper and he belonged to an artist called Francis Barraud, who dropped into the Gramophone Company (as it was then called) offices one day and asked if he could borrow one of the characteristic brass horns from a gramophone to complete a picture he had painted. He showed the people at the company the picture – a little white mongrel listening intently to the sounds coming from the horn of a dull black phonograph, just as I used to do looking down the speaker cover. Barraud

FORTUNE THEATRE

RUSSELL STREET, W.C.2   (Opposite Drury Lane Stage Door)

Managing Director	PRINCE LITTLER
Licensed by the Lord Chamberlain to	D. A. ABRAHAMS
Controller	FREDERICK G. LLOYD

By arrangement with ANNA DEERE WIMAN

WILLIAM DONALDSON   &   **DONALD ALBERY**
for
W. & D. PLAYS LTD.

for
CALABASH PRODUCTIONS LTD.

present

ALAN   PETER   JONATHAN   DUDLEY
BENNETT   COOK   MILLER   MOORE

in their revue

BEYOND THE FRINGE

Directed by ELEANOR FAZAN .

Setting and Lighting by JOHN WYCKHAM

Originally conceived and produced for the Edinburgh Festival by John Bassett

First Performance: Wednesday, 10th May, 1961

PROGRAMME - ONE SHILLING

explained that he thought a brass horn would brighten the picture up.

The powers-that-be at the Gramophone Company liked the picture and offered to buy it on the understanding that the phonograph, which was a rival contraption, was painted out and a gleaming gramophone painted in. Barraud agreed, and within a few years Nipper was on display all over the world. In fact it wasn't long before he ousted the company's old trademark and began to appear on record labels.

The only countries he didn't appear in were Moslem ones and those where dogs were generally considered to be unclean; in those countries he was replaced by the cobra symbol.

Nipper died in 1895, four years before he became internationally famous. It was said that he had been buried under a mulberry tree in Kingston-upon-Thames, and in the 1950s HMV, as the company was then called, after the title of the painting, decided to disinterr his remains and re-bury him at company HQ. When they found the spot, however, something rather sad had happened: a car park had been built over the top of little Nipper's grave.

Interesting Interpretations

Bach: Larry Adler, mouth-organist, claimed that even Bach came down to the basic suck, blow, suck, blow.

Beethoven: In Colin Davis's words, 'Beethoven is about trying to get on with your wife. It is a reconciliation of opposites.'

Counterpoint: In my experience, Davis's remark also sums up the satisfaction of certain counterpoint, combining two entirely disparate and independent tunes.

Fugue: A piece of music in which the voices come in one after another and the audience go out one after another. (Anon.)

Trombone: Sir Thomas Beecham asked a player of this instrument if he was 'producing as much sound as possible from that quaint and antique drainage system which you are applying to your face?'

Set to Music

The opening of my parody of a madrigal

When I was twelve years old I wrote a piece of music which I gravely entitled 'Anxiety'. I suppose this must have been one of my earliest attempts at composing anything autobiographical and certainly said a lot about my state of mind at the time. Writing the score a few years ago for my film *Six Weeks*, eight bars of sublime music emerged which seemed then to sum up what I felt about my life. In the intervening years a lot of music had flown under, or over, the bridge, depending on what you were playing, or how well you mixed your metaphors.

Some of the earliest compositions I ever offered to the playing public were musical parodies, popular tunes arranged in the style of famous composers. I began composing these when I was a student and they took me to cabaret, the Edinburgh Festival, *Beyond the Fringe* and later into films (I sang a 'madrigal' to myself in a mirror in *Thirty Is a Dangerous Age, Cynthia*). I only parody what I absolutely adore. That's to say, I only imitate those composers for whom I have the profoundest respect and admiration. Beethoven has served me well. Two of the parodies I've enjoyed most were modelled on his work. One was a setting of 'Colonel Bogey', the other a piano quintet created from the songs 'The Green, Green Grass of Home' and 'Delilah'. Benjamin Britten was another composer whose music I tried to emulate with a setting of 'Little Miss Muffet' in the style of his folk songs, which I tried to sing like Peter Pears, whose voice I have long admired.

As a spin-off, it's a terrific thrill now to hear my son starting to compose pieces of his own using melodic ideas reminiscent in spirit of music of mine to which I used to rock him asleep when he was little and which he whistled round the house when he was older.

Not all of my compositions have been quite as felicitous, I have to confess. In order to gain my second degree I had to compose a string quartet during that year's study. I knew I had to do the wretched thing, but there didn't seem any point in practising it all year, and inevitably it kept being put off until the last minute, leaving me in the end with three weeks to write it from start to finish. There was an element of parody in that: I couldn't afford to run the electric lighting into the small hours every morning, so a lot of the quartet ended up being written by candlelight – very rococo. I even resorted to writing a slow final movement, so that the piece would run for the required length of time, but like so much of my work it was a tight squeeze.

It comes as a slight compensation, then, to discover that I am not the only composer to have undergone a few musical bumps along the way. Some of the greatest names in musical history have been on the receiving end of some savage remarks. Others have taken other set-backs in their stride. And a lucky few have been able to raise a laugh and a smile when things haven't quite gone according to plan.

'Beethoven's Bridgetower sonata' is what his famous Kreutzer sonata might have been called if he had stuck to his plans.

Rudolphe Kreutzer was admittedly a famous violinist in his day, but his name has been etched into musical history largely by Beethoven's dedication, which came about almost by chance. At the time of composition, Beethoven had intended dedicating the sonata to a young black American violinist, Robert Bridgetower.

Bridgetower was a first-class violinist and at the time of the sonata's composition (1802) was all the rage in musical circles. Unfortunately, before the piece was printed, he and Beethoven had a violent disagreement over a young lady and the composer crossed out Bridgewater's name, replacing it with that of Kreutzer, whom, it's said, he not only didn't know, but had never set eyes on!

On being told that his violin concerto was so difficult that it needed a six-fingered violinist, Arnold Schönberg is said to have replied, 'I can wait.'

Bring on the Girls!(?)

It is sad, but true, that there is a great deal more in this book about men than there is about women.

Why are there so few women composers? Why so few women conductors?

The truth is that the role of women in music has generally mirrored their role in society in general, and it is only in this century that women have begun to assume their rightful place.

The trouble really began with Saint Paul. He never seemed very keen on women in the first place, and in one of his Epistles he said, 'Mulier in ecclesia taceat'. He might, actually, have said it in Hebrew or Aramaic, but in any language it translates as 'Let the women be silent in church.'

Now, since the most music-making at the time was taking place in church, this effectively deprived any woman with a musical talent of any outlet for that talent. True, women were allowed to sing in a convent, and there were a few women composers in the middle ages – Abbess Hildegard of Bingen (1098-1179) is the only one whose music has survived – but since men were usually not allowed into a nunnery, and it was a male-dominated society in which the men, naturally, did everything best, very little notice was taken of them.

When we reach the Renaissance, music has become more common in the home, but a woman's role was still strictly defined. In his famous work *The Book Of The Courtier*, Baldessare Castiglione sets out exactly how far a woman can go:

When she is dancing, I would not wish to see her use movements which are too forceful and energetic, nor, when she is singing or playing upon a musical instrument, to use those frequent and abrupt diminuendos that are clever but not beautiful. And I would suggest that she should choose instruments suited to her purpose.

Imagine what an ungainly sight it would be to have a

woman playing drums, fifes, trumpets, or any instrument of that sort. And this is only because their stridency buries and kills the sweet gentleness which enhances everything a woman does. So, when she is about to ... make music of any kind, she should first have to be coaxed a little, and should begin with a kind of shyness, suggesting the dignified modesty that brazen women cannot understand.

In other words, a woman should be musical for a man's entertainment, but the only thing to take seriously was looking decorous!

As we get nearer to our own times, there are a few women who fought against what must have seemed impossible odds, and began to compose. Corona Schröter was one of the first to publish, and her first collection of songs came out in 1786. However, she announced in a musical magazine that:

I had to overcome much hesitation before I made the decision to publish a collection of poems to which I provided some melodies. An attitude of propriety and morality is branded upon our sex, which does not allow us to appear alone in public, and without an escort. So, how can I present this, my musical work to the public, without timidity?

Clara Schumann (1819-96) was far from timid (she described Berlioz as 'cold, unsympathetic and querulous', and Liszt as 'a smasher of pianos'!), and she was acknowledged as one of the finest pianists of her day, but she was still bound to a great extent by the limitations imposed upon her by society. She had been, for example, a promising composer, but gave it up early in her career. This was due in part, she said, because next to the compositions of her husband, Robert Schumann, hers sounded 'effeminate and sentimental' (a view not shared by Robert), but mainly because she came to believe what society told her, that 'a woman must not desire to compose – not one has been able to do it, and why should I expect to? It would be arrogance'.

Clara was fortunate to have such a husband as Robert, for he recognized, admired and encouraged her talents. He also worried that he was holding her back. He wrote in the diary that they kept together:

Am I to neglect my own talent, in order to serve you as a companion on your journeys? Have you allowed your talent to lie useless, or ought you to do so, because I am chained to the paper and the piano? ... Thus I torture myself with thinking ... Yes, it is most necessary that we find a means whereby we can both employ and develop our talents side by side.

How many men today are so considerate?

Fanny Mendelssohn Hensel (1805-47) was the sister of Felix Mendelssohn Bartholdy (1809-47), and her musical talent was every bit the equal of his. But whereas he was encouraged by their parents to pursue a career in music to the best of his abilities, she was forced to think only in terms of the home and marriage. 'Music shall be his profession, but for you it can and should be only an ornament, never the root of your being and doing', said her father in a letter.

While he adored his sister, Felix too took this view. He did not believe that she should publish any of her works, and some of her songs actually appeared under his name. This backfired on him when he met Queen Victoria, who announced that she would sing one of his songs, while he played the piano. He himself admitted his pique when the Queen chose one of Fanny's songs! Nevertheless, he still opposed her taking talents beyond the domestic situation, and when his mother asked him to persuade Fanny to publish them, he wrote: '[but] to persuade her to publish anything I cannot, because this is against my beliefs ...', and then showing himself rather insensitive to his sister's own aspirations, he adds:

From my knowledge of Fanny I should say that she has not the inclination nor the vocation for authorship. She is too much of a woman for this. She manages her house, and thinks neither of the public, the musical world, nor even of music at all, until her first duties are fulfilled.

Even Adelaide Ann Proctor, who wrote the words to the 'Lost Chord', which Sir Arthur Sullivan set to music, did not escape criticism – even if poetry was considered more suitable for a woman. About the lines

> I struck one chord of music
> Like the sound of a great Amen

Samuel Butler wrote (ignoring such things as poetic licence!):

It should be 'The Lost Progression', for the young lady was mistaken in supposing she had ever heard any single chord 'Like the sound of a great Amen'... Fancy being in the room with her while she was strumming about and hunting after her chord!

Ethel Smyth, probably the first well-known woman composer, had to fight both her family and the establishment to use her talents. She had her own theory about the reasons that women were denied the joys and pleasures of music. She told of the legend that Adam was having his customary nap after lunch, and Eve was rather bored. She picked up a reed, and, anticipating what the Greek god Pan was later to do, made some holes in it, and began to improvise a tune. At this point Adam woke up, and yelled at her: 'Stop that horrible noise,' and then added, after a pause, 'Besides which, if anyone's going to make it, it'll be me not you!'

And that, I suppose, is why there is so much more about men than women in this book!

Washed-up concert pianist?

Not washed up at all. Robert Mann (first violin, Juilliard String Quartet) and D.Moore rehearsing for our first public appearance together in a chamber music concert at the Grace Rainey Rogers Hall at the Metropolitan Museum in New York in 1982. We had played together privately for twenty-two years before I finally decided I would risk the chilly embraces of the classical music world. Lisa, Bob's daughter, turned pages.

The piano on the beach picture was one of a set taken by *People* magazine at the time of this concert.

Playing between takes (to Mary Steenburger) on the set of
Romantic Comedy – an activity I crave on every movie. We have a
piano in the studio or a small electric piano in my trailer.

In *Unfaithfully Yours* I played Claude Eastman, an internationally-famous symphony conductor who suspects that his wife is cheating on him. I was also the victim of a perm which fried my hair so much that an hour's worth of oil and conditioner had to be applied every morning. Despite this, as the heat rose so did my hair – like some mustard and cress burgeoning through the flannel – irresistibly and infallibly. You can see the spontaneous hair aura about to take off in this photo.

Musical Hints

The story is told that the sixteenth-century composer Josquin des Prez had several times been promised a sum of money by his employer, Louis XII, which, despite a number of hints, was not forthcoming. Des Prez hit upon the idea of appealing to the king in a more original way, composing a motet to be sung before him using words from Psalm 119 and including verse 49, 'Remember the word unto thy servant, upon which thou hast caused me to hope.'

Hearing this, the king took the hint, and gave the composer his money. Josquin was obviously grateful, for he composed another motet from the same psalm, this time incorporating verse 65, 'Thou hast dealt well with thy servant, O Lord, according to thy word.'

Many musicians still spend large parts of their lives travelling and living out of suitcases, but modern transport means that they can regularly get home to see their wives and families. That wasn't true for Haydn and his musicians, who provided music for the Esterhazy family and who had to travel with the family wherever they went.

So whenever Prince Esterhazy and his retinue took off for Schloss Esterhazy in a remote part of northern Hungary, their Kapellmeister and his retainers went too, leaving their wives and families behind for months at a time. This wasn't particularly popular and Haydn, aware of some dissent in the ranks after a particularly long spell without home leave, composed his 'Farewell' symphony (number 5).

In the last movement of this piece the instruments drop out one by one, and for the first performance at Schloss Esterhazy, as each player finished his part, he blew out the candle that illuminated his music stand and crept away from the orchestra. Prince Esterhazy couldn't ignore the hint. Before long a holiday had been arranged for the musicians.

Haydn himself would not, I reckon, have been too worried at the prospect of a long period away from home. In fact he enjoyed travelling as a means of getting away from his wife, who was a notoriously difficult woman.

Once when he was away from home a visitor remarked on the tall pile of letters sitting on Haydn's desk. 'Who are they from?' he asked. 'They're from my wife,' replied the composer. 'We write to each other every month, but I don't bother to open her letters and I'm sure she doesn't open mine.'

The prime candidate for the title of Enfant Terrible of modern music must be the composer John Cage. (Even if he is now in his seventies!) The following is a selection of his works to date:

'Imaginary Landscape No. 5', for any forty-two recordings.
'Imaginary Landscape No. 4', or 'March No. 2', for 12 Radios (24 players).
'Speech', for five radios and newsreader.
'Variations IV', for any number of players, and sounds or combinations of sounds produced by any means, with or without other activities.
'33⅓', for records and gramophones.
'Child of Tree', for percussionist using amplified plant materials.
'Telephones and Birds', for three performers with telephone announcement and recordings.
'4'33"', solo to be performed in any way by anyone.

The most notorious performance of 4'33" is that of a pianist who walks on to the concert platform, opens the piano; sits at the open piano for four minutes and thirty-three seconds of silence, and then closes the piano and leaves the platform.
    Stravinsky, on hearing about Cage's 4'33", said that he was looking forward to a full-length work by the same composer!

Why Bother?

Many composers must have been distressed to learn why the great violinist Jascha Heifetz had played their music: 'I occasionally play works by contemporary composers for two reasons,' he explained. 'First, to discourage the composer from writing any more, and, secondly, to remind myself how much I appreciate Beethoven.'

Right, kids — I'm going to give 'em the old UGGER-DUGGER DUG...!

Poor Old Beethoven!

I am an enormous admirer of Beethoven and I'm mildly annoyed by people who complain about his ghost looming over music. I don't think he does really. He just seems to have been the most lively and dramatic composer to have arrived on the musical scene – the first really dramatic composer. His material may not always be as thrilling as the end result – what he manages to build from that simple motif in the fifth symphony is a case in point. I'm not fond of some of the gruffer moments in his music, or that of Brahms, but I've always been a champion of Beethoven's.

Of course he wasn't a conspicuously happy man. In fact, in his own words, 'I must confess that I live a miserable life... I live entirely in my music.'

Life was tough on him from the start. His father, probably remembering how much money Mozart was said to have earned as a 'Wunderkind', forced him to practise all day, every day. When he was eight, he put him into a public concert, and even said that his age was six – to make him seem all the more remarkable. The attempt failed. However, by the time Beethoven was seventeen, Mozart had heard him play, and had prophesied a great future for him.

Beethoven seemed unhappy about leaving it to chance though, remarking once 'I will seize fate by the throat; it shall certainly not bend and crush me completely.' Perhaps he felt that 'fate' had a dirty throat, because he soon developed the habit of washing his hands in ice-cold water before he started to compose. (He claimed that it concentrated his mind!)

Beethoven was well aware of his own worth, whatever trials he may have gone through. In a letter to Prince Lichnovsky he said: 'Prince, what you are, you are by birth; what I am, I am by myself. There are and will be thousands of princes. There is only one Beethoven.' He believed most strongly in his god-given gift. When the violinist Schuppanzigh complained about the technical difficulty of a piece, he received the reply: 'When I composed that, I was conscious of being inspired by Almighty God. Do you think that I can consider your puny little fiddle when He speaks to me?'

His last few years were not happy. He was increasingly humiliated and frustrated by his deafness, and he became more depressed the more he alienated his friends with his temper.

On his deathbed, he is said to have quoted the dying Augustus: 'Plaudite, amici, comedia finita est' – 'Applaud, my friends, the comedy is over.'

Oh, La La!

Jacques Offenbach, the man who gave the world the Can-Can, had a reputation for being a snappy dresser and a dandy. In this respect he was quite meticulous, except for one small detail: he kept forgetting to button his flies. This became such a frequent occurrence that in the end his wife worked out a secret way of telling him something was amiss. Whenever she started speaking about 'Monsieur Durand', Offenbach knew it was his cue to leave the room and make a few adjustments to his dress.

Offenbach once dismissed a valet from his service, but not without writing glowing references for the man. Seeing these, a prospective employer asked the composer whether the valet was really everything that was claimed. Offenbach assured him that he was an excellent valet in every respect. In that case why had he sacked him the prospective employer asked with justification?

'Well, you see,' began Offenbach, 'he always beat my clothes outside my door and I could never get him to do it in time.'

Charles Ives, now recognized as America's first great composer, spent a frustrating life in which his music was seldom played and only started to be appreciated as he approached old age.

His father, a music teacher and leader of the town band, may have been responsible in part for developing Ives's unique and not always acceptable musical talents.

As part of his own musical experiments, Ives senior invented a machine to produce 'quarter tones', the notes found 'in the cracks between the piano keys'; the neighbours didn't think much of that. They didn't think a lot either of the 'ear-stretching exercises' that he developed for his children, which required them, among other things, to sing 'Swanee River' in E-flat, while he accompanied them in the key of C.

Hector Berlioz – Hopeless Romantic

Berlioz, who employed what he termed an *idée fixe*, the 'fixed idea' of a recurring theme, in a number of his works was the subject of a fairly fixed idea among his fellow composers. Chopin said of him, 'Berlioz composes by splashing his pen over the manuscript and leaving the issue to chance.'

Felix Mendelssohn agreed: 'Berlioz is a freak, without a vestige of talent,' and 'His orchestration is such that one . . . ought to wash one's hands after handling some of his scores.'

To Debussy he was 'Monster'. Bizet said that Berlioz possessed 'Genius without talent', while Ravel agreed, saying that among musical geniuses, Berlioz was 'the worst musician'.

Brahms was slightly kinder, expressing the opinion that Berlioz's music was 'often rough on the ears', but he was in the minority in his generosity.

Most of this probably washed off the composer's back. He was a man who possessed a number of extraordinary talents, among them the questionable ability to name every one of the Sandwich Islands! He made little secret of the ruling passion of his life, openly admitting once, 'My life is to me a deeply interesting romance' – a fact which was borne out by a prose style which makes that of his critics positively stingy with words. He once wrote, 'My arteries quiver violently. Tears . . . indicate only a condition which may be intensified. If the further condition is reached, muscles contract spasmodically; limbs tremble; feet and hands grow quite numb . . . I cannot see perfectly; I am giddy and half fainting' – and that just came from hearing a piece of music that appealed to him! Though, once one gathers that he felt 'My heart swell, my budding imagination open wide, my lip tremble, my voice tremble and break' when he read the *Aeneid* at the age of eight, these later reactions become more understandable.

In order to support himself while studying at the Paris Conservatoire, he took up journalism and writing reviews; neither of which was to his liking. 'My brain seemed ready to burst', he wrote once, 'my blood was on fire. I felt as if burning coals were scorching my veins. I tore my hair and wept. I beat my fists against my skull . . . I want to work, and I have to toil in order to live.' That little outburst was occasioned by trying to write an opera notice. In spite of this, he still found time for his own music; among other things at the Conservatoire, he composed an opera about a gambler, a cantata about a horse, and an oratorio about an ocean.

He was as passionate about Paris as he was about his music, and missed it terribly. Writing about his time in Rome: 'I suffered agonies. I lay groaning on the ground, stretching out abandoned arms, convulsively tearing up handfuls of grass. I felt as though my heart were evaporating and about to dissolve away. My skin was burning on my body.'

Perhaps this man of undisguised emotions was best summed up by Robert Schumann, who commented, 'Berlioz does not try to be pleasing and elegant; what he hates, he grasps fiercely by the hair; what he loves, he almost crushes in his fervour.'

Music by Degrees

When Haydn visited England he was awarded the degree of Doctor of Music by Oxford University as a mark of national appreciation for his unique musical gifts. Before this could be conferred, though, Haydn was asked to go through the formality of submitting an example of his musical learning to the university. The composition he sent was for three parts, but only six bars long. However, after careful examination it was found to be a clever canon which, whether read backwards, or forwards, whether started in the middle or turned upside down, always represented a melody with the correct accompaniment.

There are lots of military bugle calls like the 'Reveille' and the 'Last Post', but none of them uses more than five notes. These calls were first collected in a single publication in 1798 and it's thought that some might have been composed by Haydn who was visiting England at that time.

Spoilt for Choice

Rossini often found himself imposed on by aspiring composers anxious for professional criticism of their work. One such uninvited 'colleague' was a young Italian who presented himself to Rossini with two compositions and asked the great man to tell him which he thought the better. Reluctantly Rossini agreed to listen and the composer took his seat at the piano and began the first. When he'd finished this, he reached for the score of the second, only to be told, 'There is no need to play further. I much prefer the second.'

I had a not dissimilar experience with some of my own compositions a few years ago. These had been transcribed from some gramophone records I'd made by a very talented musician whom I visited sometime later. While I was with her she offered to play some pieces for me and I listened with a mixture of horror and fascination as she painstakingly reproduced one of the recordings including all the mistakes I knew that I'd made when my stamina or my musical invention had given out. That was a weird and I'm sure unique experience!

The Russian pianist and composer Anton Rubinstein was notoriously difficult to rouse in the mornings, and as a result often missed his early-morning appointments. The story goes that, in despair, his wife worked out a way to get him out of bed by playing an incomplete chord on the piano. This would so annoy the maestro's sensitive ears, which couldn't bear to hear such unresolved dissonance, that he'd leap out of bed and go to the piano to complete the chord. And while he was doing this, his wife would sneakily remove the bedclothes. Wives of lazy musicians, please take note!

You cannot imagine how it spoils one to have been a child prodigy.

Liszt

Lisztomania

'An inspired charlatan' was how Herman Levi described Franz Liszt in a letter to Clara Schumann. She was even more prosaic, and called him, as we have seen, 'A smasher of pianos'. Certainly, the violence of his piano recitals was legend. A contemporary account of his concerts said that, 'Terrified pianos flee into every corner... gutted instruments strew the stage, and the audience sits mute with fear and amazement.'

His appearance was indeed wild, and his presence charismatic. Frederic Chopin said that, 'when I think of Liszt as a creative artist, he appears before my eyes rouged, on stilts, and blowing into Jericho trumpets.'

Beethoven simply called him a 'Devil of a fellow – such a young rascal!' – but then, he only knew him as a youngster.

Liszt's daughter, Cosima, was the wife of the renowned conductor Hans von Bülow. For a while, at any rate. She had an affair with Wagner, and in 1865 had a child by him.

'If it had been anyone but Wagner, I would have shot him,' said Hans, whose admiration of Wagner was undiminished by this affair.

Eventually, Cosima eloped with Wagner, had a further two children by him, and married him; a rather unconventional order in which to do things. Liszt, whose lovers included George Sand (the woman novelist), and a Polish countess who tried to poison him after he left her, was not sure if he really approved of her divorce and remarriage – especially as he was thinking about taking Holy Orders in the Roman Catholic Church. He couldn't really say anything though – he was still a bachelor himself!

When someone had the nerve to complain to Stravinsky about the scale of fees he charged for performances of his works, the composer replied, 'I do it on behalf of my brother composers, Schubert and Mozart, who died in poverty.'

It Takes One to Know One

Brahms was noted among his friends for two reasons: one, for being Germany's greatest living composer, and two, for being one of the most untidy, sloppy, messy people in the country.

One day a friend called on him, and finding the front-door open, went in. Brahms wasn't there, but the sight of papers, books, clothes and so on strewn all around with a thick coating of dust everywhere, so disgusted the friend that he wrote 'PIG' in large letters in the dust covering the piano. Some time later the two met in the street, and the friend mentioned that he had been to see the composer. 'Yes,' replied Brahms, 'I found your calling card!'

The Strausses

Johann Strauss jnr is the one who we mean when we speak about 'Strauss' – he wrote the 'Blue Danube' – a waltz which I have to confess I have never raved about. But the situation is slightly complicated by the fact that his father was also called Johann, and also wrote waltzes. Johann jnr also had two brothers, who used to write waltzes in their spare time, but Eduard was really a civil servant, and Josef invented a machine to clean the streets – so, as you can see, they were a talented family.

Strauss snr could see that Johann jnr was likely to prove great competition for him, and he tried to stop the child from having music lessons. When his debut concert came, Father even went so far as to send a group of people to boo and hiss. But to no avail. 'Good evening, Father, Good morning, Son', wrote one newspaper.

'The Blue Danube' was not successful when it was first performed. Perhaps the reason was that it had some truly appalling words when it was premiered by the Vienna Men's Choral Society. However, once they got rid of the words, the piece came into its own. At the Boston Peace Jubilee concert, in 1872, Strauss was there to conduct a performance in which there were eleven hundred players in the orchestra, with Strauss armed with a long, illuminated baton, and a hundred assistant conductors to guide them through it.

'A cannon shot sounded – a gentle hint for the twenty-thousand to commence playing', he wrote. 'I gave my signal, my hundred assistant conductors followed me as swiftly as they could, and there then broke out an unholy racket, such as I will never forget.' That is how he described it. But, for a fee of $100,000, I doubt that he complained for long.

His first operetta was appropriately called 'The Merry Wives of Vienna'; Strauss had had several of his own. His second wife, for instance, was so angry with him for marrying Mrs Strauss no.3, that she held a one-person-demonstration outside his front door, complete with a placard!

But in general, people liked and admired him. When Brahms was asked for an autograph once, he drew a few bars of 'The Blue Danube', and scribbled underneath 'Unfortunately, not by Johannes Brahms', which is as great a testimonial as one could wish for.

Ralph Vaughan Williams, as he arrived in the States, was surrounded by a crowd of eager reporters. 'Tell me, Dr Vaughan Williams,' said one of them grabbing his arm, 'What do you think about music?' The aged composer studied the man's face for a time, and then made the grave announcement 'It's a rum do!'

The Sound of Heaven...

That was the way one person described the *Miserere* by
Allegri; an appropriate sentiment as this most beautiful
piece of music was considered to be the exclusive property
of the Vatican, and the act of copying it was a crime
punishable by excommunication. Thus it remained a jewel
in the Papal crown until the fourteen-year-old Mozart
heard it during Holy Week and, immediately after the
service, reputedly wrote the whole of the complicated piece
out from memory.

It was reported feats like this that stunned the musical
world and won him such adulation. Everyone was always
asking Mozart for advice, and on one occasion he was
approached by a young man who asked for helpful hints on
composing symphonies. Mozart suggested that he start by
composing something more simple – ballads, perhaps. 'But
you wrote symphonies when you were only ten years old,'
protested the fan. 'Yes, but I didn't have to ask how to do it,'
replied Mozart. If such stories make him appear arrogant,
he had a lot to be arrogant about.

He also had a delightful sense of humour, if this story is
to be believed. It is told that Mozart and Haydn once agreed
on a challenge, the winner to receive a case of champagne,
which involved Haydn playing a piece that Mozart had
written earlier in the day. Haydn accepted the challenge,
sat down at the piano and embarked confidently on the
first bars. All went well for a few moments, until he came
to a part where the composition called for him to continue
with one hand at each end of the keyboard and
simultaneously to strike a note right in the middle.
Protesting that it couldn't physically be done, he
relinquished his seat to Mozart, who played the piece
through and, reaching the 'impossible' note, lowered his
head and hit it with his nose!

It's generally accepted that Mozart wrote the most
sublime music, but very few people realize that he was
considered one of the best billiard players around, often
composing between shots. Very few people realize, either,
that I might have followed his success on the green baize if

fate had smiled on me a little more generously, or for longer than one shot.

This was the first time that I'd played snooker. I was at the home of 'Cubby' Broccoli, the producer of the James Bond films, playing with Michael Caine and Denis Selinger. My first shot ricocheted around the table and then cracked one of the balls into a pocket. It was the sort of shot you wish you could play every time. Of course you don't play it all the time, which is why I should have stopped there and then, leaving them dumbfounded. As it was I carried on and played with total chaos. Pride comes before a fall. Maybe my career might have taken a different turn and 'Cubby' Broccoli might have seen me as the new James Bond – who knows? But back to Mozart.

Altogether he lived a remarkably full life, if a short one. It is rumoured that he once proposed marriage to Marie Antoinette. If she had accepted him, perhaps the whole history of Europe would have been different. (They were only about seven years old at the time, but 'Puppy Love' had yet to be written – one hit that slipped through Mozart's fingers.)

In his childhood, his father pulled the child prodigy around Europe on a gruelling tour. He played for nearly every crowned head in Europe, and the monarchs all showered him with gold watches, silver snuff-boxes and all manner of precious gifts. (His father would rather have had the money, but you can't look a gift snuff-box in the mouth.)

After three years touring around, they decided it was time to go home. Like all travellers returning home after a long trip, they were apprehensive about getting through customs without paying too much duty. However, they needn't have worried. Mozart senior unpacked the clavichord at the border control, Mozart junior played it, and the guards were so charmed that they let the party take all their gifts in duty free. This gave Father Mozart another reason for boasting. 'Orpheus could tame wild animals with his music,' he used to announce, 'but my boy tamed the customs officials, and that is a great deal more difficult.'

Certain composers have become renowned for the speed at which they have written a number of their most famous works. Some of the most notable instances of this quick-fire composition belong to the careers of Handel and Mozart. Handel composed his 'Messiah' in the space of twenty-three days; while his 'Israel' took only four days longer.

Mozart, however, composed his G minor Symphony in just ten days; the *Marriage of Figaro* only occupied the month of April 1786, the finale to the second act of which Mozart dashed off in twenty-four hours at a time when he was feeling so ill that before the last page or two had been scored, he had passed out in his chair. While Donizetti is said to have been in the habit of composing an entire act of an opera after dinner!

There was one thing that Igor Stravinsky loved about the United States, to which he defected from Russia – and that was whisky. He enjoyed this tipple so much that he was once heard to remark happily, 'My God, so much I like to drink Scotch that sometimes I think my name is Igor Stra-whisky'. He didn't mention whether his favourite pastime also made him see pink elephants, but he probably wondered whether he'd had just one too many when choreographer George Balanchine called him and asked him to write music for a new ballet – for baby elephants.

Stravinsky's Circus Polka Ballet is probably one of the most bizarre sights ever seen at Ringling Brothers, a Barnum and Bailey Circus – and also one of the most bizarre pieces a famous composer has been asked to write!

Sources of Inspiration

For Thomas Alva Edison genius was 'one per cent inspiration and ninety-nine per cent perspiration', but then as a scientist he wasn't taking into account some of the more unusual stimuli resorted to by those in search of artistic inspiration. Haydn, for example, couldn't compose unless he was wearing a diamond ring that had been given to him by Frederick the Great. Rossini found he had to have a glass of champagne before sitting down to write his music. Paisiello could only compose between warm sheets. Gluck went to the extreme of placing himself and his piano in the middle of a lovely meadow with a bottle of champagne on either side. Beethoven regularly doused himself with cold water. Cimarosa couldn't work unless he was surrounded by the chatter of talkative friends. Cherubini was in the habit of cutting out any blot he made while writing music and filling the gap with another piece of paper, a process that made his finished manuscripts look like a paper mosaic.

Villa-Lobos, like Cimarosa, used to like composing in the midst of his family as they played, talked and worked all around him. I've never understood how anyone can have that degree of concentration. When I'm writing I shut myself behind my door and if anyone comes in I stop. I'm getting better now, but for years I couldn't reveal that part of myself even to people I knew very, very well. Composition seems such a personal thing that I wonder too how people can collaborate on writing tunes.

The public doesn't want new music; the main thing it demands of a composer is that he be dead.

Arthur Honegger

Overture and Beginners

When the idea arose to stage a performance of Victor Hugo's play *Ruy Blas* in aid of the Theatrical Pension Fund, the committee invited Felix Mendelssohn to compose an overture and a romance for the performance. This he agreed to do, but finding himself seriously pressed for time, concentrated on the romantic music and didn't write a note for the overture. The committee thanked him, though not without commenting that it was 'a great pity he had not written the overture, though they quite understood it could not be done in a hurry, and next year, if they might be allowed, they would give him longer notice.'

Mendelssohn was a bit put out by this and started writing an overture that very evening, the Tuesday night. The following morning he had a rehearsal and the day after, on Thursday, a concert. All the same, by early on the Friday the overture was ready to be sent to the copyists. On Monday he played through it three times with the orchestra in the rehearsal room, and once in the theatre. And that evening it was given its first public performance in aid of the Theatrical Pension Fund.

Jobs for the Boys

Handel was destined to become a doctor, Wagner a painter, Schubert a schoolmaster, Schumann a lawyer and Verdi was almost made a monk. It was one Father Seletti who was responsible for directing the young Verdi's career, and it was he who realized his extraordinary talent after officiating at mass in Verdi's home town of Busseto.

The service had been accompanied by some extraordinarily beautiful music and after it had finished he asked to see the organist to thank him. To his surprise it was little Verdi who sheepishly appeared. 'Whose music were you playing?' Seletti asked. Shyly the little boy explained that he hadn't brought any music with him, but had just played what he felt like playing. 'Ah... then I advised you wrongly,' said the priest. 'You must be no priest, but a musician.'

There was I, destined to become an organist/choir master, who became a comedian. There must be some poetic justice here. My father worked on the railway as an electrician at Stratford works. I was always a little unclear as to his exact role there, but he used to produce impressive drawing-boards covered with electrical diagrams which had something to do with electrifying coaches. I remember the pride with which we used to stand on the station at Chadwell Heath waiting to catch a train, watching one of the great expresses roar past the platform like a hurricane pursued by a cloud of smuts that peppered us like lead shot. My father could tell which each of them was and I still have a great affection for trains.

So did the composer Antonin Dvořák. He spent a great deal of his time when not teaching or composing, talking to engineers, porters and drivers at Prague station. He obviously had a formidable memory: it's said that he had a perfect knowledge of the railway timetable and could often be found apologizing to passengers if a train wasn't on time.

Handel (With Care!)

George Frederic Handel was a very volatile man, whose singers crossed him at their peril. He once held a soprano, Francesca Cuzzoni, dangling out of a window until she agreed to sing a part *his* way. 'You may well be a devil,' he told her, 'but you should remember that I am Beelzebub himself!'

Cuzzoni was the great rival of another diva, Faustina Bordoni. When they were in any of Handel's operas together, he had to divide the roles exactly equally, so that each had the same number of lines as the other. In a performance of *Astianette*, they both flew at each other on the stage, and turned the opera into an impromptu wrestling match! There was even a broadsheet brought out, which advertised as giving 'The full and true account of a Most Horrible and Bloody Battle between Madame Faustina and Madame Cuzzoni', and there were rival racehorses named after each of the combatants.

It was not only with female singers that Handel had arguments. In an opera called *Flavio Olobrio*, the tenor was a man called Gordon. He did not like the way that Handel was accompanying one of his arias, and told the composer so. Handel then told the singer exactly what he thought of him, and the row grew fiercer and louder.

'If you can't accompany me any better, I'll jump on your harpsichord and smash it to pieces!' screamed the tenor.

'Please let me know when you'll do it, so that I can advertise it,' replied Handel. 'I'm sure more people will come to see you jump than to hear you sing!'

Handel could also be absolutely shameless in the way that he stole pieces of music by other composers and didn't even try to disguise the fact. When accused of having stolen material from a composer called Bononcini, he openly admitted it, and then, to add insult to injury, added, 'It's much too good for him; he didn't know what to do with it.'

I remember rehearsing a piece by Handel for a concert when I was a student and pointing out a beautiful passage to my tutor, who was conducting. He agreed that it was very fine, before casually remarking that it had actually been written by someone else.

It was at that concert that I'd been told to show up at seven, thinking it meant seven for seven-thirty. So at twenty past seven I made my way towards the hall and heard the first movement flowing out to greet me. We were a proper Handelian orchestra and there weren't many of us in the second violin section, so I got the dirtiest of looks as I slunk into my seat.

Most people agree, however, that Handel was one of the truly great English composers. Haydn said, upon hearing the 'Halleluiah Chorus', 'He is the master of us all.' When Beethoven was asked who was the greatest ever composer, he also replied, 'Handel, to him I bow the knee.' (It is true that Berlioz said that he was 'a tub of pork and beer', but that was probably sour grapes, given the sort of treatment meted out to Berlioz by *his* fellow composers.)

And if anyone tries to convince you that Handel wasn't an English composer, but a German – ignore them. Handel chose to spend most of his life in England, and compose most of his vocal works in English. And what if he did always speak English with a heavy German accent? – King George I (of England) couldn't speak any English at all!

If Music Be the Food...

Several of the world's greatest composers have shown as much interest in the kitchen as the conservatoire. Beethoven frequently made a point of preparing his own food, convinced that no one could cook it to his liking as well as he could. Paganini's cooking was said to be second only to his violin playing. While Lully never lost the pleasure he felt from slaving over a stewing pan.

Handel once booked a table for three at one of his favourite hostelries and on arriving demanded that the waiter should serve him with food for that number, announcing, 'I am the company!'

I did the same thing once in a hotel where I was staying. I couldn't make up my mind what I wanted to eat, so I called up room service and ordered for two. In due course the waiter appeared with a tray groaning with food, at which I yelled into the bathroom, 'Dinner's here, darling,' followed by a muffled sound, as if someone was replying. A pathetic attempt to hide my greed, it might have been, but it was very enjoyable gastronomically. Although, unlike Handel, I find that I eat less if I order for two!

Rossini, who prided himself on his skill at cooking rice, once waxed philosophical on the relationship between the two ruling passions in his life, observing:

The stomach is the conductor who rules the grand orchestra of our passions. An empty stomach is to me like a bassoon which growls with discontent, or a piccolo which expresses its desire in shrill tones. A full stomach, on the other hand, is the triangle of pleasure or the drum of Joy. To eat, to love, to sing, to digest – these are, in truth, the four acts of the comic opera that we call life. Whoever lets it pass by without having enjoyed them is a complete fool.

Haydn's fondness for the pleasures of the table was such that he even overlooked his wife's annoying habit of occasionally lining her baking trays with old sheets of his manuscripts. His 'Ox Minuet' was composed to celebrate the wedding of his local butcher's daughter, a gesture which her appreciative father responded to by sending the composer an entire ox – hence the title of the work.

Max Reger, no doubt aware of this anecdote about Haydn, and also something of a gourmet himself, was delighted on one occasion to receive a basket of superb trout by an admirer, as a mark of appreciation for a recent performance he had given of Schubert's 'Trout Quintet'. Reger wasn't slow to put it about after that that he planned to include the 'Ox Minuet' in his next recital. But unfortunately nobody took the hint.

Sol Fa... So Good!

Igor Stravinsky was once offered $4,000 to compose the music for a film. This he declined, saying that it was not a high enough fee, at which the Hollywood producer pointed out that this was the same sum they had paid another distinguished composer to write music for an earlier film. 'Ah, yes,' replied Stravinsky, 'he had talent. I have not, so the work will be more difficult for me.'

After much haggling, and after a much higher sum had been agreed, the producer was heard to tell a friend, 'Now I've learnt that the musical scale begins and ends with dough.'

Rimsky-Korsakov's 'Capriccio Espagnole' has a title that is half-French, half-Italian. To add to its international flavour its Russian composer wrote it in Spanish.

Spinster of Which Parish?

J.S. Bach, although most famous for his religious music, composed a great deal of secular music – cantatas specially commissioned for birthdays, weddings and anything else people cared to pay him for. One cantata he wrote was for the engagement party of a Princess Amalia, and he dedicated it to her Father:

> His Most Serene Highness, the Mighty Prince and Lord, Frederick Augustus, King in Poland, Grand Duke in Lithuania, Reuss, Prussia, Mazovia, Samogitia, Kyovia, Vollhynia, Podolia, Podlachia, Liefland, Smolensk, Severia and Czernicovia, Duke of Saxony, Julich, Cleve, Berg, Engern and Westphalia, Archmarshal and Elector of the Holy Roman Empire, Landgrave in Thuringia, Margrave of Meissen, also Upper and Lower Lausitz, Burgrave of Magdeburg, Prince and Count of Henneberg, Count of the Marck, Ravensberg and Barby, Lord of Ravenstein, and My Most Gracious King, Elector and Master.

If you don't believe me, you can always check for yourself, because the King preserved it very carefully. The dedication, I mean. Unfortunately, he lost the cantata itself, which is a shame, because it was probably very good!

I believe in Bach, the Father, Beethoven, the Son, and Brahms, the Holy Ghost of Music.

Hans von Bülow

Ashes to Ashes...

In spite of achieving acclaim in their lifetimes many of the great composers suffered periods of doubt when they questioned whether their work would survive for posterity. The critic Ernest Newman, believing perhaps in some kind of natural justice, stated that 'The good composer is slowly discovered; the bad composer is slowly found out.'

While this is not strictly true, it might have been a comfort to many musicians struggling in their garrets! Edvard Grieg was in no doubt about this natural justice: 'If there is in my music anything of lasting value it will live; if not, it will perish. That is my belief, for I am convinced that truth will prevail ultimately!'

When Beethoven was asked how he could possibly consider his Rasumovsky Quartets to be music, he replied, 'Oh, they are not for you but for a later age.'

Haydn also had a sneaking suspicion of his own worth. In a letter to a society of music lovers he wrote:

Often when I was wrestling with obstacles of every kind, when my physical and mental strength were both running low and it was hard for me to persevere in the path on which I had set my feet, a secret feeling inside me whispered: 'There are so few happy and contented people here below, sorrow and anxiety pursue them everywhere; perhaps your work may, some day, become a spring from which the careworn may draw a few moments' rest and refreshment.' And that was a powerful motive for pressing onward.

Benjamin Britten was rather more temporal about it all: 'I do not write for posterity... I write music now, in Aldeburgh... for anyone who cares to play or listen to it.'

Duke Ellington had similar thoughts: 'We're not interested in writing for posterity. We just want it to sound good right now!'

And, if he was quoted correctly, Gabriel Fauré was

remarkably calm and collected about the prospect of death
and posterity in his last words to his sons:

> When I am no longer here you will hear it said of my
> works: 'After all, that was nothing to write home about!'
> You must not let that hurt or depress you. It is the way of
> the world... There is always a moment of oblivion. But
> all that is of no importance. I did what I could: now, let
> God judge.

It is not hard to compose, but it is wonderfully hard to let the
superfluous notes fall under the table.

J.S. Bach

(Trust Bach to come up with something as polished as this. It
epitomizes the richness of his creative imagination. He wrote
once that his main purpose was to dispell sadness and bring joy
and he did this with consummate ease, or so it seemed. With
a contented life raising his family, he had the enviable ability to
produce sublime music almost to order, without any of the
apparent suffering of the likes of Berlioz.)

The Music Man

Until recent years I found the prospect of playing the classical repertoire in public slightly daunting and it took a very long time before I felt able to appear on the concert platform with the attitude 'ready or not, here I come'. Even then I wasn't without a few misgivings. Sitting at the piano in the Hollywood Bowl about to embark on Gershwin's 'Rhapsody in Blue' with the Los Angeles Symphony Orchestra I realized the reassurance Dame Myra Hess must have derived from having the music in front of her when she played in public! I could only hope to goodness that I remembered everything.

From an early age I was always so obsessed with trying to get every detail absolutely right that I never got into the habit of completely memorizing a whole piece of the music. I wanted to be a concert violinist so much when I was studying at the Guildhall that the desire itself became a major obstacle. I was so nervous at the start of one of my exams that my fingers seized up and I couldn't move them for what felt like sheer terror. My sister and I would religiously tackle the Spring sonata for violin and piano by Beethoven until six bars in I came to grief on a tricky passage and we ground to a halt. It was always the same passage where I came unstuck, but we persevered through those opening six bars time and again.

My music seemed to be comprised of fragments in those days. Nothing was ever completed. Perhaps that's why I was drawn to improvisation: you can pretend that you've finished off at any point you like and no one can condemn you for hitting the wrong notes because it's all totally fresh.

I have to be honest and admit that there was something of the lemming-like approach to music even in my improvisation, even when I was with the Dudley Moore Trio and discovering that you could play and earn money at the same time. There was an occasion when I was booked to play at a college ball in Oxford and invited a girlfriend to go with me. Only when we arrived did I remember that I hadn't booked us anywhere to stay for the night, so we spent most of the night after the ball trying to sleep in a telephone box.

Despite minor inconveniences like this, that sort of environment was where I played my best jazz. When Peter Cook opened the Establishment Club in London I used to play there every night and on the foot-high rostrum I could feel everything coming through from the bass and the drums as well as hear them. Chris, my drummer, used to get the high-hat off-beat going so hard that he turned his cymbals inside out a couple of times! We used to play like madmen there; I even had old dustbin lids beside the piano which I would throw down at the climax of a piece. The swing that happened was like a tap being turned on and I felt as if I could have played for ever. That lasted for maybe a year and then we tried to record it and the magic simply evaporated. We were never able to play quite like that again.

As a conductor there was another musical experience that came some way towards measuring up to that time at the Establishment. That was when I first conducted an orchestra playing my own music for my first solo film, *Thirty Is a Dangerous Age, Cynthia.* I could hardly speak I was so excited, and whatever my conception of it might have been the sound was so remarkable I was completely over-whelmed. Working on *Bedazzled* a few years later there was a violinist named John who puffed a cigar through the whole recording, yet played one piece I'd written so movingly that when he asked me up in the control room whether it had been all right I had difficulty in sobbing out 'Yes... yes...' For him though it was just like digging up the plants in a garden – all in a day's work.

That's probably enough about me. Let's see how other players and conductors have coped with various aspects of their professional (and in a few cases amateur) lives.

I am saddest when I sing; so are those that hear me; they are sadder even than I am.

Artemus Ward

The Amateur Singer

Few descriptions of this phenomenon can be as accurate and amusing as this, from *Three Men In A Boat* by Jerome K. Jerome...

When Harris is at a party, and is asked to sing, he replies: 'Well, I can only sing a *comic* song, you know,' and he says it in a tone that implies that his singing of *that*, however, is a thing that you ought to hear once, and then die... Well, you don't look for much of a voice in a comic song. You don't expect correct phrasing or vocalization... You don't bother about time. You don't mind a man being two bars in front of the accompaniment, and easing up in the middle of a line to argue it out with the pianist, and then starting the verse afresh. But you do expect words.

You don't expect a man to never remember more than the first three lines of the first verse and to keep on repeating these until it is time to begin the chorus. You don't expect a man to break off in the middle of a line, and snigger, and say, it's very funny, but he's blest if he can think of the rest of it, and then try and make it up for himself, and, afterwards, suddenly recollect it, when he has got to an entirely different part of the song. And break off without a word of warning to go back and let you have it then and there...

George Ade must have spoken for thousands of long-suffering families when he noted once, 'The music teacher came twice a week to bridge the awful gap between Dorothy and Chopin.'

Professional musicians run odd risks in the pursuit of their profession. As an organist I soon discovered the condition generally known as Organists' Trousers, though here I was more fortunate than some of my fellow musicians. All I suffered was a tendency from the sliding up and down on the organ bench, for the seat of my trousers to shine sooner than they might otherwise have done; I gather that professional organists can set the frequent replacement of trousers off against income tax now, which at least lends some virtue to necessity. I had a further complication when it came to playing the organ and that was my left foot, which is slightly mis-shaped and has the characteristic to turn inwards. In an attempt to correct this at the organ I used to wear the right shoe of a pair of my mother's court shoes. My left leg is also shorter than the other one, so to compensate for this I used to add almost a couple of inches of rubber heel. This enabled me to get some lift in my foot to work the pedals. To get even more lift I cut a groove in the sole, slotted a lace through this and tied it tight round the back of my leg. In the end I had a special shoe made that incorporated all these Heath-Robinson features and wore that when I played the organ at Oxford. That's until the senior college organist told me he'd found a peculiar looking shoe knocking about in the organ loft one day and had thrown it away. 'I think it must have been yours,' was his only comment!

The sort of trying conditions that afflict other musicians are classified under terms like Glissando Thumb, suffered by pianists; Clarinetist's Lip; Fiddler's Neck, which can so easily be mistaken for a love-bite (perhaps a physical expression of Orsino's opening line in Twelfth Night, 'If music be the food of love, play on' – play on indeed). Flute players can sometimes succumb to a skin reaction known engagingly as Flautist's Chin. And most alarming of all is the constant risk of contracting Cellist's Nipple, though that selfishly confines itself to female players, who understand only too well what Sir Philip Sidney was hinting at in his First Song when he talked about his 'breast o'ercharged to music'.

Anything to Oblige

Frederick Delius owed a great deal of his popularity to the untiring efforts of Beecham in promoting his music, but even this did not spare him from Beecham's irresistible urge to get the better of his professional colleagues.

Delius, sitting in on a rehearsal of a new composition of his, was asked by Beecham, during one of the breaks, whether the last passage had met with his approval. 'Yes, except for the horns, maybe,' answered Delius.

'We'll try from bar six again, gentlemen,' said Beecham to his orchestra.

'Yes, that was better,' said the composer when they'd finished.

'Good,' replied Beecham. 'By the way, Fred, you know there are no horns in that passage.'

Sign Here Please...

Today's newspapers occasionally run a story about someone who has named a poor, unfortunate child after the entire team of Manchester United Football Club, or some other sporting squad. This is not a recent madness, however. One of the most famous conductors of the nineteenth century was called Louis Jullien – or rather, he was known as Louis Jullien. His parents had christened him after all his godfathers, who were the local village band in its entirety, of which Jullien's father was the conductor. Thus his real name was: Louis George Maurice Adolphe Roch Albert Abel Antonio Alexandre Noé Jean Lucien Daniel Eugène Joseph-le-Brun Joseph-Barème Thomas Antoine Pierre Carbon Pierre-Maurel Barthélemi Artud Alphonse Bertrand Dieudonné Emanuel Josué Vincent Luc Michel Jules-de-la-Plane Jules-Bazin Julio-Cesar Jullien.

Time, Gentlemen... PLEASE!

'The Gluepot' is a nick-name which is credited by musical lore to many people, but it was probably originally coined by Sir Henry Wood. It was given by him to a public house called 'The George' in Mortimer Street, very near BBC Broadcasting House. Legend has it that Sir Henry became so used to waiting for members of his orchestra to return from refreshing themselves in this hostelry that he gave it the name 'because once they get in there, they seem to be stuck in it.'

When the Royal College of Music was built in the nineteenth century it had 98 rooms. If a member of staff could not be found, he was said by the porter to be in room 99, i.e., the nearest pub. Even after the building was enlarged, there was never a 'Room 100', and room 99 was left to denote that part of the musician's training which is not covered by the syllabus.

* * *

Divine Intervention

'God save me from a bad neighbour and beginner on the fiddle,' says the Italian proverb.

I remember mother used to suggest that I should go out into the garden and play my violin to Mrs Wilson who lived next door. Violins don't sound at their best in the open air, especially if you're none too competent on them in the first place; only now can I imagine the purgatory she must have endured as I scraped through 'In a Monastery Garden'.

You know why we conductors live so long? Because we perspire so much.

Sir John Barbirolli

What's the Problem?

Many conductors have been considered to be insensitive in all matters except music. One celebrated (and possibly apocryphal) example involved Sir John Barbirolli, who was at the time conducting the Halle orchestra. A member of the orchestra had been having a long-standing affair with a singer. All went well until the man's wife found out. She stormed into the concert hall and, after a blazing row with her husband, ran into the conductor's room in floods of tears.

'Can I help you?' asked Sir John.

'It's my husband, he's in love with this woman, and I just don't know what to do,' said the wife, choked with tears.

'My dear,' he replied soothingly, 'there's nothing to worry about, you know. His playing is better than ever.'

False Economies

A student who was anxious to study under Artur Schnabel was tested by the great man, who decided to take him on. How much were the lessons, asked the pupil. Five guineas a time, replied the maestro.

'I'm afraid I couldn't afford that,' said the pupil.

'I also give lessons at three guineas,' Schnabel told him, 'but I don't recommend them.'

Music lovers who still flock in their droves to hear The Merry Widow *have Dvořák to thank, as well as Franz Lehar.*

Lehar told the story of how his real ambition was to be a great concert violinist. He practised and practised every day, with unfailing devotion and dedication. Eventually, his good friend Antonin Dvořák could bear it no longer and told him, 'For heaven's sake, nail your fiddle to the wall, and try to become a composer.' Without this advice, Lehar always insisted, 'I would be a poor violinist, instead of a rich composer'!

The 'violin duel' scene from *Unfaithfully Yours:* highly symbolic fun stuff. In the film, I think that the character played by Armand Assante is having an affair with my wife. He persuades me to play a duet with him publicly in a restaurant, and I turn it angrily into a sort of swordfight in the best Errol Flynn/Basil Rathbone tradition.

Roger Moore was trying to persuade me to smoke a cigar. (Quick quiz: what is the connection between this photograph and what I've written in the first chapter, under the heading of 'Set to Music'?)

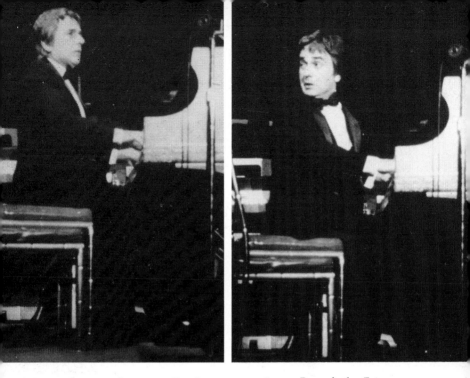

Moments from my Beethovian parody in *Beyond the Fringe*. There's a spot of relatively calm lyricism, followed by a pleading look to the wings for help as the sonata makes it clear it is refusing to end, and – finally – the futile struggle of man and music in which only panic and ignorance can survive!

'Jamming' with Chick Corea and Chuck Mangione.

Pete Morgan is on bass, and the clarinettist is Eric Lister.

Idle Moments!

The life of a professional musician is, in general, a happy
one for the musician who is in work. In his heart of hearts
he knows that he (or she) is doing something far preferable
to any of the alternative forms of employment. Nevertheless, it has to be admitted that there are long moments of
boredom – of waiting for a conductor, a recording
engineer, a priest, or a stage-manager to stop the scenery
falling on to the actors. It is probably in these moments
when the musician may question his vocation.

These times are filled in many ways: if you get a box near
enough the orchestra pit at Glyndebourne (the opera
house situated in the heart of the Sussex downs), it is
difficult to decide which is more riveting – the action
onstage, or the action in the pit. In some operas – especially
baroque and classical ones – many players may have long
periods of inactivity. The sight of a seasoned musician who,
in one continuous movement, can put down his paper –
having read it through once and begun the crossword –
pocket his pen, take up his instrument and begin playing
and be in perfect time is truly awesome. This doesn't
happen only at Glyndebourne, of course, but perhaps one
notices it more because Glyndebourne – by virtue of being
miles away from anywhere – doesn't allow its musicians to
indulge in another favourite way of passing idle moments:
nipping into the local pub for a swift half!

It is perhaps in such moments as these that the nick-
names by which various pieces of music are known are
thought up. Many of them are, naturally, drink related.
Thus, Tchaikovsky's 'Eugene Onegin' becomes 'Eugene
One Gin', Debussy's 'Clair de Lune' becomes 'Clear the
Saloon', and so on. Sometimes the retitling has its origin in
'Franglais', for example Debussy's beautiful piece 'La fille
aux cheveux de lin' is inaccurately and most inappropri-
ately translated as 'The girl with the lines of a horse'!
Others owe their inspiration more to Dr Spooner (or,
perhaps one 'swift half' too many!), as in Delius's 'On
hearing the first cuckoo in spring', which becomes the
rather more barbaric 'on cooking the first hero in spring'.

In a similar vein, though rather more self-pitying, the 'Flight of the Bumble-Bee', is usually referred to as 'The blight of the humble fee'.

Church music is also a great source of examples of this phenomenon. The great Victorian composer Sir Hubert Parry composed a glorious choral piece called 'Blest Pair of Sirens', but what floats down cathedral naves more often than not, is 'Best Pair of Nylons'. Choirboys also take great delight in re-punctuating the verses of hymns in an heretical, if not downright irreligious, fashion:
'My God, I love thee; Not because/I hope for heaven thereby...'
'My God, I love thee not. Because I hope for heaven thereby...'
or,
'Lord, for tomorrow and its needs I do not pray...'
'Lord for tomorrow and its needs. I do not pray...'

Rather more blasphemous is the re-punctuation of the great Easter hymn found neatly penned-in in all the hymn books of one church: 'Jesus Christ is Risen Today' became 'JESUS: Christ is risen today!'

Popular songs are not immune from this disrespectful treatment either – and love songs seem to lend themselves very well.

'Love is where you find it' becomes 'Love is where? – You find it!'

'What now my love?' with a subtle change of emphasis assumes the more commonplace air of exhaustion, 'What, *now*, my love ???'

And finally, the enigmatic and philosophical song 'What is this thing called love?', to which I remember Michael Caine giving a similar change in emphasis, which transformed it into an ode to the bridegroom's nightmare: 'What is *this* thing called, love?'!

After I die, I shall return to earth as the doorkeeper of a bordello and I won't let one of you in.
   Toscanini, to his orchestra at an unsatisfactory rehearsal.

Otto Klemperer

I was a student when the Otto Klemperer version of Beethoven's 'Eroica' Symphony came out and I played it endlessly because it was the most extraordinary recording I'd ever heard of anything. Along with Errol Garner's 'Concert by the Sea' and Jacqueline du Pré's recording of the Elgar Cello Concerto which came afterwards, the Klemperer 'Eroica' has remained one of my three favourites. It was the fugal section from the funeral march in this that I chose for one of my eight records on *Desert Island Discs*.

Although not such an ostentatious wit as Beecham, many stories are told about Klemperer, often referring to his eccentric behaviour on the concert platform as he grew older. At a concert in London, for example, the elderly conductor shuffled on to the concert platform, sat on the stool that was always provided for him, and took up his baton. He raised his hands, looked around the orchestra for a moment, and then put it down. After a few seconds, the orchestra became rather nervous. The leader leaned forward and whispered: 'Are you all right, Dr Klemperer?' The aged Doctor eyed him balefully for a moment, said quietly, 'What a life!', and took up his baton again.

Another story runs that Klemperer came on to the concert platform, acknowledged briefly the applause, and turned round to the orchestra. Through his open fly was displayed a large expanse of shirt-tail. After a while the orchestra leader managed to attract the conductor's attention.

'Maestro,' he hissed, 'your fly buttons are undone.' Klemperer looked at him with an air of bewilderment.

'What has dat to do wiz Beethoven?' he asked.

At a rehearsal with a German orchestra, the leader always addressed Klemperer with severe formality, and would preface each remark by reciting his official title, 'Entschuldigen Sie, Herr Doktor Generalmusikdirektor Klemperer, aber...' After enduring this for some time, Klemperer cut the man short: 'Call me Otto!' he said, wearily.

Although he survived well into modern times, conducting right until his death in the 1960s, he was essentially a man of the early part of the century – a man who had known Mahler and Strauss. His grasp of modern recording techniques was rather sketchy, and so one day an engineer attempted to explain to him how they took various 'takes' of sections of the music, and then edited the good sections together. Klemperer looked dismayed, 'So it is not my conducting, this record?'

Patiently, the sound engineer explained again that it was his conducting, but not a single performance, a performance made instead from various sections knitted together. Klemperer turned to his daughter, and shook his head in great melancholy.

'Lotte,' he said sadly, 'Lotte, ein Schwindel.'

The great man was not, however, infallible. He always maintained – mistakenly – that his true vocation was to be a composer. The young conductor Daniel Barenboim once received a summons to visit the maestro, at very short notice, in his hotel room. Barenboim hurried to see him, wondering what this could be about. When he arrived, he found Klemperer sitting there with a beautiful young soprano. The old man handed Barenboim a pile of songs – all composed by himself – and told him to start playing them, while the girl would sing.

After what seemed like hours, Klemperer motioned for him to stop.

'Well,' beamed Klemperer, 'Do you like them?'

Barenboim decided that he must be honest. 'No,' he said, 'No, I do not.'

Klemperer seemed to take the judgement well enough, and continued to chat away for a few minutes before Barenboim made his apologies, and left. As he was going out, he heard the old man say to the pretty young soprano:

'Barenboim is a nice lad. He speaks his mind, but he has no taste in music.'

One of Dr Klemperer's greatest linguistic gifts was the ability to say a great deal in one of his short, pithy witticisms. During a break in rehearsals for a concert they were giving together, Klemperer talked to the great

German baritone Dietrich Fischer-Diskau about the singer's forthcoming solo recital.

'What are you singing?' asked the conductor, 'Schubert?'

'No,' replied the singer.

'Schumann?'

'No.'

'Wolff?'

'No,' said Fischer-Dieskau once again.

'What then?'

'I'm singing Brahms.'

'That is not necessary,' pronounced Klemperer!

On another – more pointed – occasion, the conductor was attending a lecture given by the German composer Hindemith. Klemperer found the lecture long, boring and pretentious. When it eventually came to an end, Hindemith asked if there were any questions. No one moved for ten seconds, and then, very slowly, the aged Doctor rose to his feet. 'Where is the lavatory?' he asked.

However, his most brilliant off-the-cuff remark must be his reply when asked by the management of an Israeli concert hall if he would be available to conduct the *Messiah*. Dr Klemperer looked quizzical, as though some little detail had momentarily escaped his mind.

'Was there not once some trouble with your country and the Messiah?' he murmured, innocently.

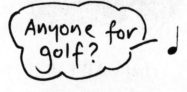

On the Ball

As well as being a master of the violin bow, in his younger days Jascha Heifetz was a mean hand with the table-tennis bat. So it was with justifiable pride that his fellow violinist Nathan Milstein used to boast that he had once beaten him, adding by way of emphasis, 'What's more, I beat him after I'd played the Mendelssohn Violin Concerto under Toscanini.'

Tuning Up

Rather like a singer or soloist giving their first recital, or an actor on the first night of a play, the first time in front of an orchestra for a conductor is a harrowing and nerve-racking affair.

André Previn was only twenty when he made his debut, in Hollywood. His additional problem was that the orchestra were all his friends, and he was unsure how to achieve the balance between discipline and friendliness. The musicians obviously sensed his unease, and when he asked the oboe to give an 'A' for the orchestra to tune-up, he was disconcerted to hear an A-flat. He was even more alarmed when he heard the members of the orchestra tuning to it, as this would result in the music being played in the wrong key. Then he noticed a few wry smiles on their faces, and – more at ease – he continued to 'study' his score until they had finished. Then he tapped his baton, looked around and commanded, 'Right, now everybody transpose a half tone up.' As he brought the baton down, the orchestra collapsed in helpless giggles, and the rest, as they say, is history.

That's All Folks!

Sir Thomas Beecham was well known for his dislike of the music of Vaughan Williams and at the rehearsal of a Vaughan Williams symphony, he seemed to be doing little more than half-heartedly beat time. He was still doing so when he realized that the orchestra had stopped.

'Why aren't you playing?' he enquired.

'It's finished, Sir Thomas,' replied the leader.

Looking down at the score, he turned over a page and found it blank. 'So it is,' he said. 'Thank God!'

The Value of Notes

The astonishing virtuosity of Niccolo Paganini had an interesting and rather unexpected impact on a reviewer who covered a concert the great violinist gave in Paris once. The critic was evidently more struck by the impressive receipts of the evening than the music that had earned them, and having enquired what the total return had been, he sat down to establish the real cost of the evening's entertainment. A sum of 16,500 francs (then valued at about £687.50) had been taken that night, and with an impressive attention to detail, the critic worked out the individual costs of each note.

Paganini had played three pieces in the concert, each covering five pages of music, with about ninety-one bars to the page. Together the fifteen pages contained 1,365 bars, by which he divided the 16,500 francs. The result looked like this:

> 12 francs for a bar (or 12 francs for a semibreve)
> 6 francs for a minim
> 3 francs for a crotchet
> 1 franc 50 centimes for a quaver
> 15 sous for a semiquaver
> 7.5 sous for a demisemiquaver

While rests were valued at:

> 6 francs for a minim rest
> 3 francs for a crotchet rest
> ... and so on

> *He was a fiddler, and consequently a rogue.*
> *Jonathan Swift*

An Impractical Demonstration

A British orchestra was rehearsing a new work by a modern French composer, under the baton of a French conductor. The maestro was unhappy with a passage being played by the clarinet.

'No, no, no!' he cried. 'Don't play it like that, but like this . . .' and he sang 'La-la-la . . . la, la . . . laaa LA.'

'Ah!' said the player, in mock surprise, you mean . . .' and also sang 'La-la-la . . . la, la . . . Laaa LA.'

'Yes, yes that's it,' the conductor said, content.

The clarinettist paused for a moment, then – through gritted teeth – said, 'Good. Now we know we can both sing it, who's going to play it?'

(I had a similar experience once with a horn player. There was one particular passage in the piece I'd written that I wanted him to bring out. When he played it though, I thought he was a little out of tune and suggested, as tactfully as I could, 'I hate to say it, but you're sounding a little sharp to me.' He noted this and we had another go, but that still wasn't right. 'I hate to say this,' I ventured, 'but it's sounding a little flat now.' 'Listen,' he replied, 'I can pull in, pull out, or push off!')

At Last!

Sir Thomas Beecham and the violinist Jean Pougnet were appearing with an orchestra which, at the rehearsal, seemed rather to be in awe of them. The start of the work was a shambles, but Beecham persevered and, after a while, the players began to come together. He leaned towards Pougnet and said, 'Don't look now, but I believe we're being followed.'

Prodigy: A child who plays the piano when he ought to be asleep in bed.

J.B. Morton

Mistaken Identity

The story is told about the composer of notoriously discordant and difficult music coming to a rehearsal one day to listen to his new work being conducted by Sir Adrian Boult. The man sat silent but impatiently for half an hour. Finally, he could bear it no more. He jumped up, crying, 'Sir Adrian, excuse me one moment,' and came to the front of the hall.

'Why, good afternoon,' said Boult, 'how nice to see you.'

'Sir Adrian, please forgive me interrupting, but couldn't you take it just a little faster?'

'Indeed we could, yes,' agreed the conductor, adding – almost as an afterthought – 'But you do realize that we haven't come to your piece yet?'

Musical Politics

A young drummer was attending his first rehearsal under Sir Thomas Beecham. Naturally, he was rather nervous, and to make matters worse the piece they were to rehearse had a drum solo in it. He asked advice from a member of the orchestra as to how Sir Thomas liked it played.

'Good and loud,' came the reply. 'You can't give him too much. He's an old man now, remember, and getting a bit deaf.'

The young man absorbed the advice, and Beecham came in. He looked straight at the new addition to the orchestra, and said, 'We will begin with the drum solo.'

Beecham watched with feigned horror as the drummer attacked his drums with all the zeal and vigour he could muster.

'Young man,' said the conductor, as the echoes fell away, 'You are not a drummer – you are an anarchist!'

Perhaps it was because Nero played the fiddle, they burned Rome.

Oliver Herford

Nut and Boult

If it was only musical problems that the conductor of an orchestra was up against each day, he could probably cope. Unfortunately behind every orchestra there is normally a small army of bureaucrats – as Sir Adrian Boult discovered when he took over as conductor of the BBC Symphony Orchestra. The BBC likes to get good value for its money, and consequently Sir Adrian had to run the orchestra on a tight budget. On one occasion a conflict arose when the powers-that-be discovered that he intended to perform a piece that required two piccolo players. He was summoned and informed that his budget allowed for only one piccolo player, and, despite protests, he was met with nothing but blank insistence that they could do nothing about it, and rules were rules.

Sir Adrian went straight to the top of the department and put the problem to the controller. Naturally enough, the department head wanted to alienate neither his conductor nor his administrators, so after a great deal of thought he came up with a suggestion that he thought might solve the problem. 'How about using one piccolo,' he asked, 'and placing it closer to the microphone?'

Sir Malcolm Sargent was well known as a 'showman' among conductors. Whereas, for example, Henry Wood had a poached egg and half a glass of mineral water before a concert, Sargent would have oysters and champagne as his snack.

When he conducted in Australia in 1936, he went to the first rehearsal dressed with his customary sartorial elegance in an impeccable suit with a red carnation in the buttonhole. The Australians were rather taken aback at this, as they had never seen anyone dressed in this way for a rehearsal. During the first break the brass section went out to a local coffee-house, and noticed a street-trader selling red toffee-apples. On their return, each of them sported one in his buttonhole!

Language Barrier

The problems encountered by many conductors working with orchestras whose language is not the conductor's is ample proof that music, as 'the universal language', leaves much to be desired.

The Swiss conductor Ansermet – though a most excellent musician – was no linguistic maestro. When he and a concerto soloist had repeatedly quarrelled about tempi, he lost his temper and exclaimed: 'Don't spoke. Don't please spoke. If you didn't like it, you went!' While to an orchestra who had been 'messing around' in rehearsal he said: 'Please look, a joke, then and now, yes very. But always, by God, never!'

Not Quite a Literal Translation, But...

The Hungarian composer Zoltan Kodaly (pronounced 'Cod-Eye') spoke no English at all, so he needed an interpreter when he came to the United States. He spoke fluent German, however, and the orchestra had a resident German speaker, who agreed to translate.

The rehearsal did not go well, and Kodaly began to lose his patience. Finally, he went red in the face, and shouted at the orchestra, 'Schweinhunde! Sie spielen wie Schweinhunde!'

The translator paused only for a second while he considered his options. 'Gentlemen,' he began, 'the Maestro admires your playing very much, but would admire it even more if you could give him a little more expression at letter G.'

Temper, Temper

Musicians, like artists of all kinds, are often very short-tempered. The conductor Koussevitsky once had a violent argument with one of the members of his orchestra, and demanded that he should leave the platform.

On his way out, the man turned round and fired a parting shot to the conductor: 'Nuts to you!'

'No,' insisted Koussevitsky. 'No, it is too late to apologize!'

Well, You Did Ask...

A certain conductor – probably Knappertsbusch – was conducting a rather second-rate orchestra in Germany. At the reception after the concert, the sycophantic chairman of the orchestral board compounded the unpleasantness of the evening by monopolizing him in conversation.

'Tell me, Maestro,' the chairman asked, 'when was the last time you conducted our orchestra?'

'Tonight,' came the strained reply.

Going by the Clock

A certain well-known conductor was renowned for his rather confusing technique of not beating time, but simply making circles with his baton – faster or slower according to the music. One new player in the orchestra confided in his fellow musicians that he couldn't follow this at all, and had no idea when to begin or stop playing.

'Don't worry about it,' said one of the more seasoned members of the band, 'just do what I do – get ready at quarter past, and start playing at twenty to.'

*　　*　　*

Beating Retreat

For an orchestral musician Fürtwängler's beat at the podium was far from encouraging, consisting as it did of little more than a convulsive tremble. On the occasion of his debut at La Scala, this idiosyncracy was still unnerving to the players seated in front of him, and as he started to shake all over just before taking them into the overture, the leader leant across and whispered, 'Coraggio, Signore!'

Novel Mystery

A very rich and remarkably untalented amateur conductor used to hire major symphony orchestras for his own amusement. Most of the players, knowing who was paying their wages, were prepared to tolerate being told how to play by this complete lack-talent. One day, however, the percussionist reached breaking point, and in a very quiet passage released his frustration by hitting everything in sight – drums, cymbals, timpani, glockenspiel – everything.

Quietly seething, the conductor laid down his baton. 'All right,' he said, 'who did that?'

Social Contract

The famous violinist Fritz Kreisler was once asked by a New York society hostess how much his fee would be to perform in her home.

'A thousand dollars,' Kreisler replied.

'Very well,' said the lady. 'But you won't be required to mix with my guests.'

'In that case,' said the violinist, 'I shall only charge you five hundred!'

Curl up and Die!

At one performance of a Mozart piano concerto, neither the pianist nor Sir Thomas Beecham gave a very good performance. In the interval the librarian asked Sir Thomas if he should leave the piano onstage, or take it off.

Beecham thought for a little while, and then said, 'Oh, leave it on. Anyway, it will probably slink off by itself.'

F Off

The story is told of an oboist in an orchestra being conducted by Rossini, who played an F-sharp instead of the F that was required. Pointing out the error to him Rossini said with understanding, 'In regard to that F-sharp, don't worry about it; we'll find somewhere else to fit it in.'

My mother used to say that my elder sister had a beautiful contralto voice. This was arrived at not through her ability to reach the low notes – which she could not do – but because she could not reach the high ones.

Samuel Butler

All Musicians Are Equal

Seldom have Karl Marx's principles on egalitarianism been applied so accurately to the arts as in the case of Russia's post-revolutionary 'First Symphonic Ensemble' (Pervyi Simfonicheskii Ansambl), known by the nickname Persimfans, which for ten years from 1922 to 1932 performed works of the utmost complexity and to the most exacting standards, without the assistance or direction of a conductor – except when guest conductors were invited to 'appear' with them.

In putting into practice Marx's ideals, the Persimfans chose to impress on the musical world that in a state where all men were considered equal, there was no need for an orchestra to be kept under the dictatorial baton of a conductor. In his place they substituted individual concentration of a high degree, painstaking attention to the playing of others – and a committee. This small group met to agree certain fundamental details like volume and tempo. Their conclusions were conveyed to the others and during rehearsals one of the committee would sit in the auditorium and monitor what went on, to report back when the piece was finished.

Yet in spite of the problems they might have been deemed to have inflicted on themselves, the Persimfans fared remarkably well, winning praise from composers and soloists with whom they worked, and gaining a loyal and appreciative following at home and abroad. After a decade though, the system started to show its cracks as individual talents began to rebel against the rigid corset within which they had been playing and the artistic experiment of the Persimfans was brought to an end by its disbanding.

Pierre Monteux, when into his eighties, signed a twenty-five year contract as principal conductor of the London Symphony Orchestra, but only on the condition that he could have an option for another twenty-five-year term when the first had been completed!

Roar of the Greasepaint – Smell of the Crowd

One way and another I've had quite a lot to do with the music of the stage and screen, and even with opera, though to a much lesser extent.

From composing music for plays when I was a student I graduated to being a resident composer at the Royal Court Theatre and writing music for the Royal Shakespeare Company, which included working on plays like *Serjeant Musgrave's Dance, One Way Pendulum* and *The Caucasian Chalk Circle.*

When it comes to the screen, in addition to writing the music for several of my own films, I also composed it for a number of others including the film version of *Inadmissible Evidence.* There was a time when I was commissioned to write the music for a documentary film about Chicago and turned up for the recording session with the terrible sinking knowledge (hello, lemmings!) that there was one music cue for which I hadn't managed to write anything. I will always be grateful to the director who didn't bat an eyelid when the cue came and I had to mumble my apologies; generously he suggested that a piece from somewhere else in the score would work 'just fine'.

My exposure to opera, as a performer at any rate, has thus far been restricted to the amateur stage, although at the age of twelve I did understudy one of the parts in Benjamin Britten's work for children, *Let's Make an Opera.* As seemed to be typical of me I didn't know the part in its entirety and if I'd ever had to go on, I'd have been fumbling and stumbling through at least the last third of it, not knowing where I was supposed to be or what I was supposed to be saying or singing.

From the point of view of listening to opera my first inclination was towards either very early or very late works: Monteverdi, Purcell, Gluck, or Benjamin Britten were favourite composers of mine. Only in later life have I grown to accept and enjoy the excesses of the opera that came between, as I suppose I've allowed myself to feel the excesses of age and music!

So, on with the show.

Beginner's Guide to Wagner

Just over a century ago the enthusiastic Wagnerites Hans and Ernst von Wolzogen published an English version of their handbook to Wagner's Ring cycle which bore the encouraging title *Guide Through Wagner's Ring*.

If enthusiasm were all that were needed to impart the deeper meaning of this monumental work, the von Wolzogens' book would no doubt have become a classic. As it was however, English readers found their earnest efforts to explain the intricacies of the plot and score as murky as the waters of the River Rhine itself. A few examples from the *Guide* will illustrate what I mean:

The bird warns again and again, when Mime with his old praise of his education, with the dusky harmonies of the cooking motive, and the coaxing-crawling motive, or even with the charming tune of Nature's life, tries to obtrude his poisonous brewage upon the dragon killer . . .

But to what end all precaution? As Siegfried with scorn and menace refutes the Walhall theme which is held up against his impatience, there in the second half of the scene, Wotan's motive of wrath rises more and more, and between its most urgent repetitions cites – in vain – the horrors of fiery blaze.

With the accords of the Walhall-march the proud passage of the godly power once more rises and then descends in several repetitions of the world's destruction, closely following each other. Her lay becomes dark and low: 'Holda's apples' are cited in vain. Gloomily the Walhall-theme dies away, the Rhinegold slowly arises in Wotan's resigned mind.

Thereupon ceases this excitement and a new lively, pompous symphonic set begins.

For the last time we hear Siegfried's motive, but the wild rush of the Götterdämmerung motive overpowers it with the utmost force: flames cover the picture of the old gods and the melody of salvation through love waves *dim*. Under ethereal harp sounds, as the freed and blessed

spirit of love of the whole world's tragedy ascends to the
eternal regions of his heavenly home!

How wonderful opera would be if there were no singers.
Rossini

Movie Music

I suppose as a musician I have very fixed notions about
individual pieces of music which are generally not very
visual. This means that when they are suddenly allied with
something to look at in films, for example, the music seems
to be diluted, which can often be mildly aggravating.

This isn't always the case. Occasionally I've seen
examples where the music and the image on the screen
have worked very well together; Bergman's *Autumn Sonata*
is a case in point. There's a scene in that in which Liv
Ullman, the daughter, is playing a Chopin prelude. Ingrid
Bergman, her mother, is sitting next to her and you see the
two of them across the piano. The mother complains that
her daughter's become sentimental, or tragic, with the
piece, which prompts the daughter to reply that her
mother has never agreed with anything she's ever done. So
mother plays the piece, and the subtlety with which the
interpretation changes from daughter to mother was
handled with such understanding of the music that it added
a superbly crafted dimension to the scene and an understanding of their relationship. I just wish this was more
often the case.

Frequently the music used remains anonymous until the
credits at the end, so here are ten examples of 'movie music'
which you may, or may not, have readily identified when
they reached your ears from the sound-track.

Barry Lyndon	'Sarabande' (Handel)
Death in Venice	Symphony no.5 in C minor – adagietto (Mahler)
Elvira Madigan	Concerto for piano and orchestra no.21 in C (Mozart)
The French Lieutenant's Woman	Sonata in D – adagio (Mozart)
Kramer vs. Kramer	Concerto in C major for mandolin, strings and harpsichord (Vivaldi)
Rollerball	Toccata in D major (Bach)
Sunday Bloody Sunday	*Così fan Tutte* (opera) Act 1 (Mozart)
2001: A Space Odyssey	'Also Sprach Zarathustra' – symphonic poem, op.30 (Richard Strauss)
Young Winston	'Caractacus' – cantata, op.35, march (Elgar)
Zardoz	Symphony no.7 in A, op.92 – allegretto (Beethoven)

Librettos for Sale

Lorenzo da Ponte, the librettist for Mozart's operas *Don Giovanni*, *The Marriage of Figaro* and *Così fan Tutte*, started a new life in America in the early 1800s, running a grocery shop in Elizabethtown, New Jersey.

In the year that Liza Minelli won an Oscar for her performance in Cabaret, *Diana Ross was a strong challenger for the award for Best Actress with her memorable portrayal of Billie Holliday in* Lady Sings The Blues. *But even if she failed to win the Academy Award itself, Diana Ross set one memorable milestone with her first movie role: in contending for Best Actress she became the first black person ever to be nominated in that category.*

Music in its Roar

When Byron published the fourth Canto of *Childe Harold's Pilgrimage* in 1817, the 'roar' he referred to was of course the sea, but the birth, exactly forty years later, of Louis Baptiste Pujol, heralded a different interpretation of his phrase. Pujol's musical 'roar' was a very personal one, some might say intimate, and in the closing years of the nineteenth century it earned him a fortune and both appalled and enthralled Parisian audiences as he performed a series of 'recitals' under the name of *Le Petomane* – from the verb *peter*, to fart!

Nature endowed Pujol with the extraordinary ability to break and control his wind in a variety of musical feats, either with the muscles of his anus alone, or assisted by a small flute. His was an act which Paris of the gay nineties took to its heart and at the height of his fame Pujol was earning two and a half times as much as Sarah Bernhardt, the leading actress of the Paris stage.

She was a singer who had to take any note above A with her eyebrows.

Montague Glass

A Matter of Diction

One of the cast in Jerome Kern's production of *Show Boat* had the tiresome habit of rolling her r's, and didn't endear herself either to the composer by complaining about the moves he gave her in rehearsal. 'You want me to cr-r-ross the stage,' she announced at one point. 'And how am I supposed to get acr-r-ross the stage?'

'Why don't you just roll on your r's?' suggested Kern.

*   *   *

I Feel Pretty

Some years after I left Oxford a production of *West Side Story* was staged at the Playhouse theatre, the stage-door of which opens on to an alley and leads almost directly into the bar of the Gloucester Arms, which stands only a matter of feet away.

One night, in about the middle of the run, Maria and Tony had given each other the green light on stage and the girls were skipping among the rails of dresses singing 'I feel pretty' when they were joined by an unexpected and unscripted reveller. Into the middle of the New York dress-shop lurched a very well-oiled gentleman of the road, in search of somewhere to spend the night. Seeing that he wasn't alone, either on stage, or, from peering into first rows of the stalls, in the house, he decided to join the girls from Puerto Rico in their fun.

Dressed as he was, he didn't look that different to some of the male members of the cast and few of the audience realized that anything was amiss until a body of Sharks appeared from the wings and hustled their uninvited guest out of Maria's place of work and back into the winter night.

The Oxford Playhouse gave me my first taste of a real stage. I was two and a half years through my course and half-way through my final year when I first trod its boards – hardly the most opportune time from the point of view of my studies. I had a solo spot in a revue in which I had to react to a recording of Julie London singing 'Cry Me a River'. I made my entrance backing on to the stage, listening to the song and reacting to the audience, which I enjoy more than anything else; I'd far rather react than speak, which is maybe what most people would wish of me! The thrill of getting laughter from this dumb-show was enormously exciting and rewarding and I got drunk on the feeling. This didn't escape the notice of my tutor who sent me to the President, the head of my college, ostensibly for a dressing down. But after establishing that I was spending a good deal of my time in the theatre and that I was greatly enjoying it, we fumbled around in a devastatingly English way punctuated with comments like, 'Yes ... yes ... yes ...

Well, I expect ... yes ... that you could make some sort of
career out of that ... yes ... I'm sure you could ... yes ...',
until he finally dismissed me saying, 'Yes ... yes ... good.'

My tutor was less sanguine and in the year when I was
working for my second degree he forbade me to go on
stage. However, the 'roar of the greasepaint – and the smell
of the crowd' kept me well, if covertly, occupied and the
string quartet on which I should have been working ended
up being crammed in at the last minute.

The Answer Lies in the Soil
(Or Underneath It)

Among his many operettas Offenbach wrote *The Divided
Turnip*, *Lady Apple*, and *King Carrot*, but his most celebrated
was *Orpheus in the Underworld*, which possessed its own rich
vein of earthy humour.

In keeping with its classical theme, the auspices for its
opening were far from reassuring. The censor was worried
by the fact that Jupiter looked disconcertingly like
Napoleon III, and after a gas-main burst the première had
to be performed by candlelight.

The fate of the production hung in the balance until the
gods smiled on Offenbach in their curiously ambivalent
way with mortals, and inspired an influential critic to
announce that the whole evening had been immoral and 'A
profanity of sacred and glorious antiquity.' That made
Orpheus in the Underworld an immediate hit, bolstered in no
small measure by the introduction of the dance which has
ever since embodied the spirit of 'gay Paris' – the Can-Can.

I once played Orpheus in a student production which I
enjoyed enormously. As he is the leader of an orchestra it
meant that I could play the violin on stage as well as sing.
Not being able to play or sing too well is a good
recommendation for the part, both of which no doubt
contributed to my casting.

The Value of Experience

Mozart's opera *Don Giovanni*, based on the story of Don Juan, owed much of its early success, on which its fame was built, to the attention to detail that its composer paid to it – in every respect. During the time that he was working on it, Mozart received the valuable assistance of a distinguished old gentleman, one Signor Jacopo, Chevalier de Seingalt, who acted as a kind of honorary consultant – a role in which he was well versed under the name that had made him famous in his younger and more red-blooded days – Casanova.

The opera written, Mozart was equally diligent in rehearsals. He was determined that the cast should act as well as they sang and here he and the soprano singing the part of Zerlina didn't see eye to eye. Time after time, he found himself berating her for the whimper that came forth when Don Giovanni made advances to her. What Mozart wanted and what the part demanded was a full-blooded scream.

In the end he decided that actions would speak louder than words and at their next rehearsal of the scene, Mozart crept up behind the lady and grasped her round the waist at the given moment. This achieved the desired effect. All reserve was cast to the wind and a perfectly executed scream greeted Mozart's improvisation. 'That,' he said reassuringly, 'that is the way an innocent maiden screams when her virtue is threatened.'

Walt Disney's Fantasia *was the first movie to have a score recorded with stereo sound, referred to as 'Fantasound'. This innovation and the film's obvious visual appeal thrilled Disney, though he wasn't selfish in anticipating its success. After watching the rushes of the part where the centaurs are cantering about in time to Beethoven's Pastoral Symphony, Disney exclaimed to one of his crew, 'Gee! This will make Beethoven!'*

'I liked your opera. I think I will put it to music.'
                    Beethoven's comment to a fellow composer

Making Overtures

Beethoven only wrote one opera, but he compensated for
the lack of further full-length works for the stage with the
number of overtures he wrote for that single work.

He set out with the intention of calling his new work
Leonore and duly set about writing an overture for it, the one
we now know as 'Leonore No. 1'. However, the story goes
that he played it through for a few friends who were so
disparaging that he had another crack, writing 'Leonore
No. 2'. (His friends' response may have been due in part to
Beethoven's rather off-hand attitude towards them at
times; he once described his friends as 'Instruments upon
which I play when I please.')

'Leonore No. 2' had been finished by the time the
manager of the theatre where it was destined to have its
first performance decided to change the title to *Fidelio*.
Beethoven was against this and out of pique insisted that
the overture should remain as 'Leonore'. In the event, he
might as well have saved his breath, because the whole
opera turned out to be a flop, described by one critic who
attended the first night as 'having no melodic ideas and no
originality.'

Six months later, he tried to have it staged again, with a
few cuts here and there, and he changed the name back to
Leonore. He also wrote the overture we know as 'Leonore
No. 3' – the famous one with off-stage trumpet calls. When
the opera opened again, the critic said of it:

'All impartial judges agree that never has anything been
written that is so ill-knit, disagreeable . . . and so revolting
to the ear, with such bitter modulations following each
other in appalling cacophony.'

All the same, the public seemed to rather like it, but
Beethoven had a row with the manager after the second

night, took away his score and refused to allow any more performances ever again – or so he said.

Eight years later, a Viennese opera director decided to revive *Leonore*. Beethoven set about re-writing it once again, and decided that he wanted yet another new overture. Unfortunately he fell asleep while composing it (the night before the opening), so the impresario had to use a different overture that Beethoven had written for a concert some years earlier. And this time, the opera was a success.

However, Beethoven never wrote another opera, and thereafter referred to *Fidelio* as 'My crown of martyrdom.'

Hired Hands

During the last century there developed an accepted tradition in many continental opera houses of hiring a claque to lead the rest of the audience in their applause, and possibly give them the impression that they were enjoying themselves more than was actually the case. These groups of 'hired hands' were frequently very well organized and for a set sum would fulfil their appointed roles with dedication and enthusiasm. For a modest outlay an artist could obtain the services of someone to shout 'Bravo!' Applause and bursts of really enthusiastic clapping (which was more physically demanding) came a little dearer. And shouts of 'Encore!' were pricier still.

Some enterprising claquers went to extraordinary extremes to attract attention to their paymasters. The story is told of one who had the good fortune to find two one-armed men, one with a left arm, the other with a right, whom he engaged to join forces (and hands) in periodic bursts of well-orchestrated applause during one memorable performance.

All singers have this fault: If asked to sing among friends they are never so inclined; if unasked, they never leave off.

Horace – Satires

The Power of Music

'Extraordinary how potent cheap music is' wrote Noël Coward in *Private Lives* and judging from the backing that advertisers frequently give to their commercials it isn't only cheap music that has the power to attract attention. The classics have been combed for suitable melodies to complement everything from aftershave to chocolate bars. Some are immediately recognizable; others are familiar, but in this unusual context hard to pinpoint; and there are some that escape the listener's memory entirely by their curious blending with the goods they are promoting. I wonder for instance what strange attraction led the promoters of Cool Footspray and Guinness independently to settle on Tchaikovsky's fantasy overture 'Romeo and Juliet' for promoting their wares?

The list here highlights just a few of the themes taken from the classics and other serious music to be used on the soundtracks of British commercials. But it's the same in other countries. Now, how many of these would you get?

Baco foil	Tchaikovsky	*1812 Overture*
BL Roadtrain	Wagner	Prelude, Act 3, *Lohengrin*
Burley aftershave	Prokofiev	*Romeo and Juliet*, ballet
Coalite firelighters	Mendelssohn	Symphony no.4 in A
Cusson's Imperial Leather	Mozart	Piano Sonata no.11 in A
Dubonnet	Canteloube	*Chants d'Auvergne*: 'The Shepherd's song'
Fiat Mirafiori	Verdi	*Rigoletto*: 'La Donna e mobile'
Gas	Mozart	Concerto for piano and orchestra no.21 in C
Heinz spaghetti	Beethoven	'Für Elise', Bagatelle no.25
Hovis	Dvořák	Symphony no.9 in E minor
Leycare	Grieg	*Peer Gynt*: 'In the hall of the mountain king'
Lux toilet soap	Fauré	Pavane
Myer's beds	Bach	Toccata and fugue in D minor
Niblets	Tchaikovsky	*1812 Overture*
Old Spice	Orff	*Carmina Burana*: 'Primo Vere'
Schweppes Malvern Water	Elgar	Symphony no.1 in A flat
Sharp's Extra Strong Mints	Dvorak	Humoresque no.7
St Bruno	Elgar	*Enigma Variations*: 'Nimrod'
Texas Instruments (watches)	Mozart	*Eine Kleine Nachtmusik*
Wool Marketing Board	Pachelbel	Canon and Gigue in D
Young's Seafoods	Schubert	Symphony no.8 in B minor

The theme music that Isaac Hayes wrote for the movie Shaft *in 1971 cut through the rock music world like a laser beam, which was reflected in popular music for the rest of that decade.* Shaft *won Hayes an Oscar, four Grammy awards and a Golden Globe. Over three million copies of the double album were sold in three months; the single reached number one in the States and number four in the UK; London's Metropolitan Police used a* Shaft-*inspired backing on one of its television recruiting drives; and I used it too as inspiration for a piece of music I had to write for television at the time.*

Fooling Around

George Grossmith, best remembered today for *The Diary of a Nobody*, which he wrote in conjunction with his younger brother Weedon, was a leading member of the D'Oyly Carte opera from 1877 to 1889, during which time he played in many Gilbert and Sullivan operettas, and 'created' the parts of Bunthorne, Jack Point, Ko-Ko and Major Stanley. All in all he was a player who knew what he was doing. So it was understandable that he got a bit fed up during rehearsals for one production of *Iolanthe* in which Gilbert, who was directing, spent an absurdly long time fussing over a tiny detail of the blocking. In the end frustration got the better of Grossmith, who complained in exasperation to his fellow players that they'd been through that move at least twenty times already.

'What's that I hear, Mr Grossmith?' asked Gilbert.

'I was just saying, Mr Gilbert, that I've rehearsed this confounded business until I feel a perfect fool.'

'Well, perhaps we can now talk on equal terms,' quipped Gilbert.

'I beg your pardon?' said Grossmith.

'I accept your apology,' replied Gilbert with a triumphant smile.

National Pride

Taking a curtain call after a performance at Covent Garden, the great Australian diva, Dame Nellie Melba, was delighted to hear rising above the applause and cries of 'Encore!' the voices of expatriate countrymen calling her name. 'They're shouting Auntie Nellie, Auntie Nellie,' she exclaimed excitedly.

'I rather think, madam, that what they are shouting is Martinelli, Martinelli,' whispered Sir Thomas Beecham.

Opera – Some Thoughts

Opera: A play representing life in another world, whose inhabitants have no speech but song, no motions but gestures and no postures but attitudes. All acting is simulation, and the word *simulation* is from *simia*, an ape; but in opera the actor takes for his model Simia audibilis (or *Pithecanthropos stentor*) – the ape that howls.

> The actor apes a man – at least in shape;
> The opera performer apes an ape.

Chorus: In opera, a band of howling dervishes who terrify the audience while the singers are taking breath.

Ambrose Bierce

Opera in English is, in the main, just about as sensible as baseball in Italian.

H.L. Mencken

I don't mind what language an opera is sung in so long as it is a language I don't understand.

Sir Edward Appleton

A Voice in a Million

Among the most unusual talents to emerge in the American musical world in the first half of this century was that of a Pennsylvania heiress named Florence Foster Jenkins. Once in a while the music master at school used to play us one of her records, so I became aware of her 'artistry' at an early age.

Following a taxi crash she found herself the owner of a voice which was now capable of reaching an F higher than she (or anyone else) had thought possible (or desirable). Equipped with this and a fat wallet, she set out to share her unique gift with fellow music-lovers in a series of self-promoted concerts and recitals throughout the country's well-heeled sections of the north-east. Behind her trooped a following of disbelieving critics and fans who expressed their appeciation of the 'diva' in delightfully ambiguous notices and comments. Robert Lawrence, writing in the *Saturday Review*, observed, 'Her singing at its finest suggests the untrammelled swoop of some great bird.' *Newsweek* was perhaps a little more candid in one review which read, 'In high notes, Mrs Jenkins sounds as if she was afflicted with low, nagging backache.' While for another critic her voice embodied 'a subtle ghastliness that defies description'.

Unswerved by praise or parody the lady continued for several years to stage musical evenings which have seldom been matched in musical history. Perhaps the highlight of her career came the year after fortune smiled on her in that taxi, when she performed to a packed house in Carnegie Hall. Shunning the visible fact that she would not see seventy again, she treated her audience to a dazzling array of guises which included the Queen of the Night from *The Magic Flute* and a Spanish coquette archly sporting a jewelled comb and red rose in her hair. As this latter apparition she treated her audience to her show-stopping rendition of 'Cavelitos', in which she punctuated each verse by throwing rosebuds from a basket, into the stalls – an inspired piece of business that only went wrong once, when she sent the whole basket flying into the house.

They That Go Down...

There's an amusing story behind the composition of Purcell's anthem 'They that go down to the sea in ships', famous for its low D which is the source of much anxiety to ordinary bass singers.

The composition arose after the maiden voyage of a yacht commissioned by Charles II (which he'd named *The Tubbs*, an affectionate tribute to the Duchess of Portsmouth), which took place round the coast of Kent. Among those invited to join the royal party was Gostling, the basso profundo of the Chapel Royal, whom the king had included so that he could entertain them all with a few songs. However, before anyone had time to start making requests, a fearful storm blew up and king, courtiers and all were called on to lend a hand at the sails while the yacht was brought safely into harbour.

The experience had such an impact on Gostling that he asked his friend Purcell to set a selection of nautical passages from the Bible to music that would complement his fine voice. Purcell did just this and the range of very low notes are a fine indication of the magnificent quality of Gostling's singing.

Movie Madness

In their enthusiasm to cash in on the popularity of the big band sound Hollywood executives placed the musicians in some bizarre positions. To fit Woody Herman's band into *Winter Wonderland*, the producers planted them in the backwoods of Canada!

The hero in a Tommy Dorsey movie, *The Fabulous Dorseys*, found himself plagued by a musical theme he had been commissioned to write, but couldn't compose. Inspiration finally broke through to him while he was sitting at a table with his girl and for some reason he hit a few conveniently placed glasses of water, which produced the tune he'd been searching for.

The girl is Katherine Healy, who starred in *Six Weeks*. She has since won much acclaim in her ballet career.

Playing during recording of the filmscore I wrote for *Six Weeks* – the music is very precious to me. An exciting and rewarding time.

Six Weeks

Arthur – no bumps on this one, please

Jazzing somewhere

It was in another Dorsey movie that one of the most ridiculous Hollywood manipulations occurred. Up on the screen showing *Las Vegas Night* appeared the band consisting of seven brass players, five on saxophones and a rhythm section, while over the soundtrack the audience were treated to the sounds of a full string section!

I suppose it's understandable that musicians should be particularly aware of details like this. I recently saw Paul Muni in *We Are Not Alone* which was being shown on television and there was a scene in which he played a violin in a spare moment between being a doctor. The violin had obviously been tuned for him off-set, but after plucking the strings to check that everything was ready, he double-checked on the piano and played the wrong note! Happy that all was ready, he wandered into the next room from which the sounds of a wonderfully sentimental tune, played beautifully on the violin, immediately followed. How they let that go I don't know!

Not that my own films have been totally free from slips like this. In *10* I can see myself in certain long-shots playing the piano in the bar, hitting the keys a moment or two before the chord comes up on the sound-track. The timing went a bit haywire in some shots in *Unfaithfully Yours* too, when I was conducting and the music track didn't quite coincide with my actions. But that's one of the consequences of being a 'miniaturist', I suppose.

The nineteenth-century French opera composer Daniel François Esprit Auber, was a man who wrote many successful works, but never attended performances of any of them. He was even less inclined to hear the works of the many upstart composers who sought his advice, and after looking through the score of one work by a precocious young composer whose 'originality' had far outstripped his age, Auber commented, 'This boy will go far, when he has had less experience.'

Clothes were something of a passion for John Christie, the founder of Glyndebourne Festival Opera. His wardrobe at one time boasted 180 handkerchiefs, 132 pairs of socks and 110 shirts. Not content with those he once found himself the owner of 2,000 pairs of plastic dancing pumps which he soon realized exceeded even his sartorial demands. He tried offloading the surplus on to fellow members of Brooks's club, but without great success. It's said that for months after their appearance, discarded plastic dancing pumps were turning up all over the club's elegant premises.

The Beggar's Opera?

John Gay's masterpiece, *The Beggar's Opera*, was a smash hit from day one. It was also a showbusiness story written in the classic mould, with the author finding success and wealth after having his piece rejected by leading theatre managers and impresarios of the day, including the great Colley Cibber. In fact John Rich was only persuaded to take the piece into his theatre in Lincoln's Inn Fields after considerable hesitation. But, in the words of the popular saying that sprang up, he made an unbeatable decision, and *The Beggar's Opera* 'made Gay rich, and Rich gay'. Poor

Handel was nearly driven into retirement as he saw his audience spirited away and found himself performing oratorios to near empty concert halls. While the smartest theatregoers, the king, queen and princesses among them, crowded into Rich's Theatre to relish the adventures of Macheath and Polly Peachum.

The returns for the first fifteen nights speak for themselves, and the fortune Gay went on to make from his work can be reckoned from noting that the third, sixth, ninth and fifteenth performances were all author's nights, when he took all the proceeds!

	£	s.	d.		£	s.	d.
Night 1	169	12	0	Night 8	157	19	6
Night 2	160	14	0	Night 9	165	12	0
Night 3	162	12	6	Night 10	156	8	0
Night 4	163	5	6	Night 11	171	10	0
Night 5	175	19	6	Night 12	170	5	6
Night 6	189	11	0	Night 13	164	8	0
Night 7	161	19	0	Night 14	171	5	0

	£	s.	d.
Night 15	175	8	0

Variations on a Theme

One evening a lady in the audience at New York's Metropolitan Opera House, leant over the front of the stalls and asked the conductor, 'I wonder whether you would be able to play the third act before the second tonight? My friend and I have to catch a train, you see, and we do so want to know how it all ends.'

The opera is like a wife with a foreign title – expensive to support, hard to understand, and therefore a supreme social challenge.

Cleveland Amory

Byron on Singers

In *Don Juan* Byron fires a couple of broadsides at singers,
saying of the men:

> The tenor's voice is spoilt by affectation,
> And for the bass, the beast can only bellow;
> In fact, he had no singing education,
> An ignorant, noteless, timeless, tuneless fellow.

When it came to the prima donna, he spared her little
either:

> though a little old
> And haggard with a dissipated life,
> And subject, when the house is thin, by cold,
> Has some good notes.

Common Sense

If she can strike a low G or F like a death rattle and a high F
like the shriek of a little dog when you step on its tail, the
house will resound with acclamations.

Berlioz, on an opera singer of his aquaintance

> *Swans sing before they die;*
> *'twere no bad thing*
> *Did certain persons die*
> *before they sing.*
> *Samuel Taylor Coleridge*

Fame and the Spur

One of the most famous *castrati* of the eighteenth century was the Italian singer Carlo Broschi Farinelli, whose voice enraptured Europe and won him fame and wealth among its royal courts. Farinelli was outstanding among singers of his age (other *castrati* included). It was claimed that his voice could reach and sustain seven or eight notes that did not exist in other voices.

So great was his impact on the royal heads of Europe that Louis XV of France presented him with his portrait set in diamonds as a token of appreciation, while Philip V of Spain engaged him to sing four arias nightly for the rest of his life, a commission that kept Farinelli busy for ten years until the king's eventual demise. Under Philip's successor, Ferdinand VI, Farinelli's voice won him even greater honours, including the rank of prince and an annual pension of £2,000.

But what are wealth and success when balanced against . . . ?

Turn Away from your Evil Ways

The music for the first comic opera was written in 1639 by two Italians called Mazzocchi and Marazzoli, which is pretty funny for a start. The man who wrote the words was called Giulio Rospigliosi, who was so ashamed of himself — or his name — that he gave up the theatre altogether and became Pope Clement IX.

During a rehearsal for a performance of Messiah, *Sir Thomas called the proceedings to a halt, and said to the chorus: 'When we sing, 'All we like sheep have gone astray', could we have a little more regret and a little less satisfaction?'*

Tales from the Footlights

Everyone involved with the theatre enjoys telling stories about things that have gone wrong on stage, and I'm no exception. There was an incident when I appeared as one of three Roman soldiers on a school stage during my student days, when we toured almost anywhere that would have us. At one point one of us had to say 'Yeh, blimey. I had to go off and have a piddle' or something like that. The point was that at the mention of 'piddle' the pupils in the audience started tittering. We tried to wait for them to quieten down, but in the meantime began spluttering ourselves – at least two of us did. The third soldier was a very serious Latin scholar whom I'd never seen laugh and who I don't believe had ever laughed in his life. It was just bad luck for me that he picked this as his first afternoon. As we two were bursting to have a good laugh on stage and the kids were rolling in their seats, this man started to crack like a monster in the finale of a Hammer horror film. The director was hissing to us to spit out the next line, but we were deaf to his pleas in the mounting hysteria.

Opera isn't free from these catastrophes either and two of the most celebrated episodes in its history are concerned with *Tosca*. The first involves the soprano playing the title role who, according to the version I heard, was a rather temperamental lady who had upset the stage-crew. At the end of the opera, she is required to throw herself off the battlements of a fortress, because her lover has been shot.

On this occasion, the stage-crew had removed the pile of mattresses on to which she would jump, and put in its place a trampoline! It is said that after 'committing suicide' in the depths of her despair, *this* Tosca bounced back into view above the battlements over a dozen times.

The other story is perhaps even more horrific. In this production a group of students were recruited to play the chorus – in this particular opera, mainly soldiers. As usual, the producer was more concerned with the principals, and left giving the soldiers their instructions until a few minutes before the curtain. 'You march on as a firing squad, line-up here, and shoot.' When they asked how they were to get off the stage, he told them 'Oh ... just follow the principals.'

In the third act, the firing squad came in on cue, but instead of aiming for her lover, they pointed the guns at Tosca herself. None of the signs she attempted to give them were understood, and they fired at her. They were rather perturbed when a man standing some distance away fell down dead, while the person they had 'shot' continued singing even louder than before! But even worse was to come. As far as they could see, Tosca herself was the only principal left onstage. So, when she threw herself over the battlements, they looked at each other, and with a shrug walked towards the same spot. The curtain came down to the sight of a platoon of soldiers throwing themselves – lemming-like – over the edge.

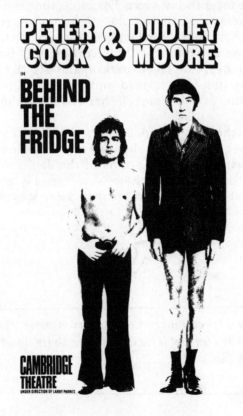

Pink of Perfection

If you were a famous nineteenth-century soprano, the toast of every city you sang in, adored by men, sought-after by high society, what would you make of this compliment? 'Madame, I have cried twice in my life. Once when I dropped a wing of truffled chicken into Lake Como, and once when for the first time I heard you sing.' Is it in fact a compliment or a backhander?

The words were uttered by Rossini when he met Adelina Patti, the most famous soprano of the last quarter of the nineteenth century. And yes, it *was* a compliment, despite all appearances, as he went on to prove by rewriting the role of Rosina (in *The Barber of Seville*) for Patti!

In the early years of this century Patti was asked to record her magnificent voice. For a long time she refused to do so, worried that on wax she might not be good enough to sustain her reputation. Finally she was persuaded to give it a try, and the moment the recording was finished she begged to hear it played back again. As the recording soared out her face relaxed and she blew kisses at the gramophone, praising herself, her voice and the record to the skies.

Despite the lack of modesty the producers knew they were on to a winner. Patti became one of the most famous and successful recording artists of the day, and was even accorded the ultimate honour — a specially printed and coloured label for her own records. Hers was pink!

Nothing can be more disgusting than an oratorio. How absurb to see five hundred people fiddling like madmen about Israelites in the Red Sea.

Sydney Smith

The Experience of a Lifetime

A young girl went to audition for a famous singing teacher in Paris (or Vienna, or Berlin, depending on where you heard the story!). When she had sung to him for a while, he stopped her and said 'You have a sweet voice, but it sounds so innocent. Are you a virgin, my dear?' The girl admitted that she was. 'Then go away, and experience life. To be an artiste you must know suffering, and you must know love. When you have, come back to me, and I will make you a great singer!'

The next morning there was a knock on the door. It was the young girl. 'Can I come in?' she asked. 'It's all right now.'

When a Nightingale Sang...

Jenny Lind, the great opera singer, known as the Swedish Nightingale, was so popular that when she sang in London, the crowds blocked the street outside her home and begged her to sing to them. And three times the House of Commons was without a quorum and could not sit because so many MPs had gone to hear her!

The doctor said he'd never seen varicose veins like them!

I know I have a reputation for bad tempers, but I am always having good tempers.

Maria Callas

All Work and No Play

The word *opera* means (in Latin) 'works', which is literally what you get if you go to see one – the works. No other art form requires so much effort, both from the performers *and* the audience. Much of the effort that the audience has to make is straining the imagination to make the plot remotely believable. As Ed Gardner said 'Opera is when a guy gets stabbed in the back, and instead of bleeding, he sings.'

Indeed, W.H. Auden maintained that 'No good opera plot can be sensible for people do not sing when they are feeling sensible.'

James Agate found that he was 'ravished' by opera, but 'on condition that I have only a vague idea of what it is about.'

Some people agree with him in this, and the best way of ensuring that natural ignorance is not tampered with is to make sure that the opera is sung in any language except English. (Many others disagree with this, however, and insist that it is impossible to hear any words anyway, and that guessing what language is being sung is half the fun.) Habitual operagoers can often be heard lamenting that things have changed, and that opera 'isn't what it used to be'. This is nothing new. In 1933, Noël Coward observed, 'People are wrong... it is what it used to be. *That's* what's wrong with it.' (*Design for Living*.)

Certainly, the historical evidence would suggest that little has changed. In 1775, the writer, Hannah More, made the observation that, 'Going to the Opera, like getting drunk, is a sin that carries its own punishment with it, and that a very serious one.'

But perhaps the best advice was given in 1882 by George Bernard Shaw, after he had seen a production of Gounod's *La Rédemption*: 'If you will only take the precaution to go in long enough after it commences and to come out long before it is over, you will not find it wearisome.'

The Unkindest Cut

I love the work of Richard Rodgers. His music for shows like *Pal Joey*, *Oklahoma*! and *The King and I* is the kind of classic Broadway material which they don't seem to be able to write any more. But everyone makes their mistakes, even Richard Rodgers. And one of his was a show entitled *Chee-Chee*, which was based on a book about life in a harem.

The story revolves around the attempts of the Grand Eunuch's son to avoid having the kind of operation that put his dad in his position – the unkindest cut of all, some might say.

It's unlikely stuff for a musical and it didn't go down too well, running for only 31 performances. But there is one moment in the score when Rodgers reveals his sense of humour – and possibly his sense of the ridiculous. At the point at which the hapless hero is being taken away to be prepared for promotion, he includes in the score a few very appropriate bars of Tchaikovsky's *Nutcracker Suite*.

Take Note

After the first performance of Mozart's *Marriage of Figaro*, the Emperor Ferdinand took the young composer aside and, giving him the benefit of his unique command of musical criticism, confided, 'Far too noisy, my dear Mozart, far too many notes...'

'If I had the power, I would insist on all oratorios being sung in the costume of the period – with a possible exception in the case of the Creation.'

Sir Ernest Newman

Horror-torio

Dame Joan Sutherland was to sing in a performance of the *Messiah* to be conducted by Sir Adrian Boult. Her husband – the conductor Richard Bonynge – had written a new and very florid cadenza for her to sing during one of the arias. She forgot to inform Sir Adrian of the fact, and at the first rehearsal it took him by surprise.

'Ah,' he was heard to mutter, as it ended, '"the Mad Scene" from Handel's *Messiah*.'

The original title for the Beatles' second film was Eight Arms to Hold You, *later changed to the rather snappier* Help!

(John Lennon actually made a solo appearance on a very early Not Only But Also *show, playing a lavatory attendant with Peter Cook and me, and also reading some of his own poetry.)*

Music in the Air

My own roots in popular music have always been in rhythm and blues, though there are lots of singers today whose music I enjoy very much.

My first job, with the Vic Lewis Band, took me on a tour of North America and provided my first taste of the New World which later became my home. I was thrilled to be there. The smell of the place struck me; maybe it was the air-conditioning. I loved the sound of the phones ringing too. I remember going into a restaurant all by myself and trying oysters for the first time, and trying to keep one oyster down while gulping like mad and trying to think of England and cricket. It was experiences like that which led me to stay on after the tour had ended, to try my luck playing in a bar in Greenwich Village.

I lived in the YMCA which was a colourful experience. Everyone there seemed to be furious about something or other. Even buying a paper from the newsagent at the corner of the block was always rather a terrifying experience. The way he came out with the *New York Times* made me feel I was trying to buy something far more intimate or indiscreet. That's how I hit the American music scene on my own for the first time at any rate.

America was also the birthplace of the greatest jazz musician to influence me – the pianist Errol Garner. I first heard him playing on a 78 when I was sixteen, and was immediately captivated. Here was a man who couldn't read music playing with a harmonic invention that was really rich and delicious to listen to and with such a subtle rhythmic approach no one has ever been able to reproduce it with total success. I thought I got somewhere near it when I was up in Edinburgh once, aged nineteen or twenty. I kept playing and became strangely speechless when people approached me for fear that I'd lose the style.

Playing in the Establishment club some years later I might have had the chance of showing how much I really admired his playing if cruel fate hadn't intervened and not for the first time sent me chasing after the lemmings.

Errol Garner came into the club and stood in the corner. I saw him and under normal circumstances might have invited him up to play, or at least done something special myself to acknowledge his presence. However, a few minutes earlier I'd spilt Coca Cola all over the centre of the keyboard from Middle C to the next C, right in the area where you can't avoid playing most of the time. The wood of the keys had swollen and the entire octave was now jammed solid like a brick. So I was having to play on either side and certainly couldn't ask him to come and take over. This was another occasion when a longed-for moment evaporated in front of me.

After one of the less august insights into my experience in the business of playing popular music, here are some glimpses into how others have fared.

In the Beginning

A report in the *Daily Sketch* on 25 September 1956 read: 'A 24-year-old labourer who kicked in a pane of glass in a greenhouse said in a statement: "I am sorry I broke it. It's just rock, rock and roll." He signed the statement "Teddy Boy", Exeter magistrates were told, but mis-spelt the signature.'

I'd like to think that when I sing a song, I can let you know all about the heartbreak, struggle, lies and kicks in the ass I've gotten over the years for being black and everything else, without actually saying a word about it.
                    Ray Charles (one of my favourite singers)

Another Foot in Another Mouth

All famous men had to start somewhere. In Irving Berlin's case, his early job was working as a waiter in a rather shabby restaurant, in the Bowery district of New York. In the corner of the restaurant was a battered old piano, on which Berlin would play after he had finished work. This piano was preserved, and became a feature of several guided tours.

Years later, after he had made a great deal of money, and become world-famous as the composer of such songs as 'White Christmas', 'Always', 'How Deep is the Ocean?', 'Top Hat', and 'Easter Parade' (to name but five!), he had a fit of nostalgia one day, and felt an urge to go back to the grotty restaurant. He was surprised to find the old piano there, still in the corner, and went over to it, sat down and began to play.

While he was playing, lost in memories, one of the tourist groups came in with their guide, who told them that on this very piano, Irving Berlin had composed some of his most famous songs. 'In fact,' he said, 'listen – the song that Bowery bum is playing now is one of his.' Then he went over to the piano, tapped Berlin on the shoulder and told him, 'Say you! If Irving Berlin could hear how you're murdering one of his greatest songs, he'd turn in his grave.'

Among the musicians of America's big dance bands baseball was a major interest. Apart from following the professional leagues, the musicians formed their own sides and played frequent matches against each other. Tommy Dorsey even went to the extent of engaging Grover Cleveland Alexander, the famous pitcher who held the record for winning 373 games, to coach his band's team and Pat Malone, another pitcher, was hired as team coach to Muggsy Spanier's band.

It's interesting that cricket has had a similar appeal to many musicians in England. Neville Cardus used to write about both and more recently Tim Rice has been successfully active in both.

Musique Militaire

Topping the charts in the early years of recorded music were military bands, in Britain principally the band of the Coldstream Guards. With the Boer War out of the way and the First World War still to brew, military bands were well placed to capitalize on the growing popularity of this new form of home entertainment. In addition to their usual repertoire of marches, military bands recorded dance music, arrangements from popular operas, and music for special occasions such as weddings and marches.

The Great Little Band (I think that's what it was called) used to be a favourite band of mine. In particular I liked their version of 'Down Among the Dead Men' which was great fun harmonically. I loved the rich tuba sound they gave it, like a stain or wash that pervades the entire quality of the music.

Led Balloon

When Keith Moon, drummer with The Who, heard Robert Plant, John Paul Jones, Jimmy Page and John Bonham playing, he said that their music would have all the success of a lead balloon. They suspected that he was right – after all, no one in the history of rock music had made a noise quite like theirs before. When the time came to name the group they remembered his comment and christened themselves after the biggest lead balloon they could think of, a Zeppelin. To make sure that there were no mispronunciations of 'lead' they removed the *a*. They needn't have worried. With the release of their first LP they became rock superstars, and the rest, as they say, is history. In fact it was their music which inspired an aptly-named music journalist called Lester Bangs to come up with a phrase that described a whole new breed of rock music – heavy metal.

Ancient Musick

The lyrics of the folk song 'Drink To Me Only With Thine Eyes' were originally written by the Athenian poet Philostratus, who lived two centuries before Christ. They were translated into English by Ben Jonson in the year that Shakespeare died, 1616.

One Lump or Two?

If you were in the UK in October 1969 you won't have been able to avoid hearing a catchy little song called 'Sugar Sugar' by The Archies. You remember it?

It was one of those tunes that goes round and round inside your head even when you wish it wouldn't. But can you remember seeing The Archies? If you say yes, you're imagining things, because The Archies didn't exist, despite the fact of sitting at number one in the pop charts for eight weeks. The Archies never actually appeared on television or in public because they were just a group of session musicians who had been gathered to record music for a children's comic strip show called *The Archies*. Quite unexpectedly they found themselves at the top of the charts!

Rock 'n roll band names often have an interesting evolution. Did you know, for example, that Steppenwolf took their name from the novel of the same title written by Herman Hesse; that Duran Duran named themselves after the villain in Jane Fonda's sci-fi movie, Barbarella; that Kid Creole's name was inspired by the Elvis Presley movie King Creole; or that Frankie Goes To Hollywood took their name from newspaper publicity about Frank Sinatra's first venture into the movies?

Lough's Luck

One of the most famous records ever made in Britain, Ernest Lough's 'Oh, For The Wings Of A Dove', was cut almost by accident. It was released in 1927 after HMV, who had created a mobile studio out of a Lancia van, had covered a recording session at London's Temple Church. A whole series of records had been cut, but at the end of the day the engineers still had two of the wax discs on which recordings were made left over. Deciding that they might as well use all of them, they asked Ernest Lough, who was a choirboy at the church, to sing for them. He obliged with 'Oh, For The Wings Of A Dove' and the record was duly released, without any promotional publicity of any kind. Within weeks Lough's pure tones had made the song a best-seller and each Sunday crowds packed the church just to see him in the choir. Even more ironic, the critics praised the standard of the disc's production, noting its excellent quality – and never suspecting that it was an impromptu performance by a boy who, until that time, had been thought of as just an ordinary choir boy!

Years after I fell in love with Ernest Lough's voice from listening to this record at home, I had the good fortune to be put in touch with his son, Robin, who was working with the BBC. He was kind enough to provide me with a cassette of his father singing this and a variety of other pieces, and told me about the extraordinary conditions in which this famous recording was made. He also made the interesting point that Ernest Lough was fourteen at the time of the recording, so he was singing with a very mature voice that couldn't have been far off breaking, which gave a special quality to his performance.

The popular Irish ballads, 'When Irish Eyes Are Smiling', 'Mother Macree', and 'My Wild Irish Rose' were all written in America.

Singers' Sayings

I wish we'd won the Eurovision Song Contest, but there's not much else I'd change.

Mick Jagger

It has sometimes been said that I don't sing very well. But where would I be if I did?

Maurice Chevalier

I love Beethoven, especially the poems.

Beatle humour from Ringo Starr

Do you remember when everyone began analysing Beatle songs? I don't think I understood what some of them were supposed to be about.

Ringo Starr, 1969

'Like sex is the thing today, you know, so I try to write a little something hinting at sex. Like one song I wrote, "Kay got laid and Joe got paid".'

Tina Turner

I heard somebody say that all black people got rhythm. Bullshit.

Ray Charles

Cole Porter received this admonition from Irving Berlin: 'Listen kid, take my advice, never hate a song that has sold a half-million copies!'

I don't know anything about music. In my line you don't have to.

Elvis Presley

Louis Armstrong was once asked by someone eager to categorize him, 'Are you a folk singer?'
    'Folk singer?' he mused, 'Guess I must be. I ain't never heard a horse sing.'

The Birth of Bop

Bop derived from bebop, which in turn grew out of classical jazz, and it made its first sounds of life in Minton's Playhouse, a Harlem nightclub around 1942.

Minton's was haunt of a group of young jazz musicians which grew to include names like Dizzy Gillespie (trumpet), Charlie Christian (guitar), Kenny Clarke (drums), Thelonius Monk (piano), and Charlie Parker (saxophone). They were looking for a new way of expressing their jazz and bop was the style they hit on. Asked once by a news reporter to define bop, Gillespie's answer was simply, 'It's just the way my friends and I feel about jazz.'

To give expression to that feeling, they started naming arrangements created in their jam sessions by the onomatopoeic formulas that reflected how each began, so 'be-bop', 're-bop' and 'oo-bop-shbam' came into being. And from them the one term 'bebop' became accepted as the nickname for the whole wave of new jazz that exploded after the Second World War. And from 'bebop' came 'bop' and later 'bopper', terms that are still used, though with different connotations, forty years on.

The Beatles recorded two versions of their first hit single 'Love Me Do'. One featured the drumming of the recently recruited drummer Ringo Starr, the other a session drummer named Andy White, brought in by George Martin who produced the record. On the version in which White took over the drums Ringo shook a tambourine.

(George Martin produced the first records I made, including the one of Beyond The Fringe, *and Andy White played the drums with the John Dankworth Band who I played with before getting involved with* Beyond The Fringe.*)*

Musical Sums

Lots of bands have numbers in their titles – test your memory and see if you can do this musical sum! (Answer at bottom of page.)

(? TOPS × ? DEGREES) – THE JACKSON ? = ?

Before making it big in the music business in his own right, Lieutenant Lush appeared with Bow Wow, the band managed by Malcolm McLaren of Sex Pistols notoriety. 'Lieutenant Lush?' I hear you say. Never heard of him? You have, you know. These days he's better known as Boy George.

Lili Millione

During the Second World War, Lale Anderson's recording of 'Lili Marlene' became the first German disc to sell a million copies, a figure which must nearly have been matched by Allied cover versions, for the song became a firm favourite in a number of different forms.

That blessed kitten has been on the keys again!

Answer: = 7 (4 Tops; 3 Degrees; Jackson 5)

Best Sellers

The first version of a previous Beatles hit to reach the British charts was Peter Sellers' recording of 'A Hard Day's Night', delivered as an imitation of Laurence Olivier's performance as Richard III, which climbed to number fourteen in the winter of 1965/66.

Peter and I appeared together in the film *Alice's Adventures in Wonderland*. He was always giggling and was great fun to be with, and I remember we were constantly breaking up during the shooting over a silly 'Knock Knock' joke:

> 'Knock, Knock.'
> 'Who's there?'
> 'Sam and Janet.'
> 'Sam and Janet who?'
> 'Sam 'n Janet evening...'

For some reason this tickled our fancy and we used to keep on singing 'Sam 'n Janet evening' in mildy Goon, or in my case sub-Goon voices.

Unsung Hero

Hard as it may be to understand now, Rod Stewart started in the rock music business by being rather shy of singing on his own. He played the harmonica and sang in the backing vocals with Jimmy and the Dimensions, his first band, and his contribution to the first hit record with which he was involved was also playing the harmonica on Millie's 1964 hit single 'My Boy Lollipop', which reached number two in the UK charts.

Animal Magic

How many records made in the last twenty-five years can you think of that have animals of some form or another in their titles? There have been a surprising number, several of which have climbed high in the charts. This list gives an indication of the range of our fellow creatures that have inspired musicians over the years, together with the names of some of the artists who have appeared on the records.

Albatross	Fleetwood Mac
Alley Cat Song	David Thorne
Ant Rap	Adam and the Ants
Baa Baa Black Sheep	Singing Sheep
Bird Dog	Everly Brothers
Birds and Bees	Warm Sounds
Boll Weevil Song	Brook Benton
Butterfly	Andy Williams
The Caterpillar	Cure
Chihuahua	Bow Wow Wow
Dance of the Cuckoos	Band of the Black Watch
Dog Eat Dog	Adam and the Ants
Donkey Cart	Frank Chacksfield
Falcon	Rah Band
Fox on the run	Manfred Mann
Funky Gibbon	The Goodies
How Much Is That Doggie In The Window?	Lita Roza
Ladybird	Nancy Sinatra
The Lion Sleeps Tonight	Tight Fit
Little Donkey	Nina and Frederick
Little Red Monkey	Frank Chacksfield
Little Red Rooster	Rolling Stones
Little White Bull	Tommy Steele
The Love Cats	Cure
Mockingbird	Carly Simon and James Taylor
On the Wings of a Nightingale	Everly Brothers
Pretty Flamingo	Manfred Mann

Puppy Love	Donny Osmond
Rabbit	Chas and Dave
Seagull	Rainbow Cottage
Shock the Monkey	Peter Gabriel
Skylark	Michael Holliday
Tie Me Kangaroo Down Sport	Rolf Harris
Tiger Feet	Mud

Starting on the Streets

Louis Armstrong started his life blowing his own trumpet in the red light district of New Orleans, and he was paid the princely sum of 15 cents a night for doing so.

Another performer who started on the streets was the tragic Billie Holiday, who was a prostitute before her famous voice was discovered. Working on the streets and getting to know what life can really be like seems to make all the difference to so many musicians – and when Billie Holiday sings 'Love for sale' in that individual voice of hers, no one can be in any doubt that she knows *exactly* what she's singing about.

In 1956 Elvis Presley recorded seventeen titles that made the charts, including five US number ones. So phenomenal was the impact he had on the music world that song writers would do almost anything to get him to record one of their numbers.

An indication of the effect of landing a Presley recording comes from the Leiber and Stoller composition 'Hound Dog'. Mike Stoller was one of the fortunate survivors from the sinking of the Italian liner Andrea Doria *and landing back in New York after the ordeal he found his colleague, Jerry Leiber, waiting on the dockside to greet him. But Leiber's mind was on more pressing matters than his friend's lucky escape from the clutches of the deep. His first words to him were, 'Elvis Presley's recorded "Hound Dog"! Elvis Presley's recorded "Hound Dog"!'*

Dressing for the Job

When the gramophone first came to Britain it was the music hall stars of the day who were most enthusiastic about recording for it. Their powerful voices and robust songs, used to filling whole theatres, were ideal for the still rather primitive equipment. Such greats as Marie Lloyd, George Robey, Dan Leno and Vesta Tilley were successfully recorded – and so was a performer called George Mozart – but not before he'd caused uproar in the studio by disappearing when he was due to sing, and returning to stand before the gramophone's huge horn in full costume, complete with make-up, red nose and wig. It had to be tactfully explained to him that to appear on a record, full costume was not strictly necessary...

Sing Up, St Winifred's

The choir of St Winifred's School probably restricted their musical repertoire to that normally associated with primary schools, and their performances to a gathering of admiring parents for the occasional carol service or end-of-term 'concert'. That's until they sang the backing vocals to Brian and Michael's 1978 British hit single 'Matchstalk Men and Matchstalk Cats and Dogs', about the painter L.S. Lowry. That reached number one in the hit parade.

Two years later, at Christmas 1980, St Winifred's were at it again, this time singing on their own, and again climbing to the number one spot for two weeks with the song 'There's No One Quite Like Grandma'.

They had one more shot at releasing a single the following year but that came to nothing, leaving them with the impressive statistic of being the only artists whose appearances in the charts have been with two number one singles.

More Musicians' Musings

If you're in jazz and more than ten people like you, you're labelled commercial.

Herbie Mann

Composers should write tunes that chauffeurs and errand boys can whistle.

Sir Thomas Beecham

Musicals: A series of catastrophes ending with a floor show.

Oscar Levant

Hot can be cool and cool can be hot, and each can be both. But hot or cool, man, jazz is jazz.

Louis Armstrong

You got to have smelt a lot of mule manure before you can sing like a hillbilly.

Hank Williams

My sole inspiration is a telephone call from a producer.

Cole Porter

There are a number of performers and bands who've been signed up first and foremost because they look the part, with their musical expertise taking a back-seat, in the eyes of some promoters at any rate. In the late fifties, Fabian was rumoured to have been discovered while sitting on his front doorstep and was snapped up by a sharp-eyed manager because he looked like a teenage idol!

More recently Sigue Sigue Sputnik have done much the same thing, having been signed up for a reputed £4 million. For, in addition to their musical talent, they convinced the executives of their record company that looking right was also a sure sign that they were going to become stars.

Music and Morality

If there used to be one sure way of guaranteeing success in American showbusiness, it was securing a slot on the famed Ed Sullivan Show. One appearance on this premier programme was said to earn an artist twelve months of bookings across the country. So it must have come as a blow to the Elvis Presley camp when Sullivan told them, 'Nothing in this great, free continent could make me put that boy on my programme.' But that was before Steve Allen, Sullivan's rival on another network, booked the rising young star and won higher viewing figures as a direct result. The following week Elvis was paid the highest fee then paid by Ed Sullivan to make three appearances on his show; though Sullivan covered himself (and Elvis) by telling his cameramen to shoot him from the waist up — a fact that Sullivan wasn't slow in broadcasting to the media. The result was that the rock 'n roll star's first Ed Sullivan appearance recorded what were then unprecedented ratings from captivated and conservative audiences alike.

Jackson Seven

It's common in the pop world to take two or three singles from a hit album, but the record for the number of singles lifted from a single album goes to Michael Jackson. Not only is his *Thriller* album the best-selling LP ever recorded, but a record seven tracks have been lifted from it and released as singles in America.

Paul Simon wrote 'Homeward Bound', the song that gave him and Art Garfunkel their first song in the UK top ten, while sitting on the platform at Widnes railway station in Cheshire, waiting for a train. At the time he was working his way round the UK playing in clubs and picking up work where he could find it.

Mistaken Identity

A man went into a music shop and asked if he could order a copy of a song called 'Could I but express in song.' Two weeks later, he received a postcard from the shop, which read:

Dear Sir,
    I regret to inform you that we can find no trace of Kodaly's 'Buttocks Pressing Song'.

Dead Beat

Three years before the Beatles took the music world by storm and ushered in the Swinging Sixties in their inimitable way, the BBC reflected its own acute awareness of the trend in popular music. After the decision to ban pop shows like *Wham! Dig This* and *Oh Boy!*, a corporation spokesman explained, 'The teenage vogue for beat music and rock 'n roll is over. Now the demand is for pop music shows of a broad family appeal.'

Cream Puns

In 1967 Cream recorded their hit album *Disraeli Gears*, the first of their albums to sell over a million copies. How many people questioned the origin of the title, I wonder? How many worked out that it was really a pun on the derailer gears found on racing bicycles?

The popular Neapolitan song 'Funiculi, Funicula' was written to mark the opening of the funicular railways running to the top of Mount Vesuvius.

> *Blind Faith, the band formed by Eric Clapton after Cream had
> played their last concert, recorded one album of the same name.
> This got to number one in both the US and UK album charts,
> the first and only time that an act has gone straight to the top
> with a debut disc, never to record again.*

A Song for You?

Girls' names have been popular song titles for years and
here is a selection that have been recorded within the last
quarter of a century, with the names of their singers.

Alison	Linda Ronstadt
Amanda	Stuart Gillies
Angie	Rolling Stones
Annabella	John Walker
Barbara Ann	Beach Boys
Billie Jean	Michael Jackson
Candida	Dawn
Caroline	Status Quo
Carrie	Cliff Richard
Carrie-Anne	The Hollies
Charmaine	Bachelors
Clair	Gilbert O'Sullivan
Cindy Oh Cindy	Eddie Fisher
Claudette	Everly Brothers
Clementine	Bobby Darin
Debora	T. Rex
Diana	Paul Anka
Eloise	Barry Ryan
Emma	Hot Chocolate
Georgy Girl	Seekers
Hazell	Maggie Bell
Jane	Jefferson Starship

Jeanette	The Beat
Jeannie, Jeannie, Jeannie	Eddie Cochran
Jenny Jenny	Little Richard
Julie Ann	Kenny
Juliet	Four Pennies
Layla	Derek and the Dominoes
Lorraine	Bad Manners
Louise	Human League
Maggie	Foster and Allen
Margot	Billy Fury
Maria	P.J. Proby
Marianna	Gibson Brothers
Marie	Bachelors
Mary Anne	Shadows
Mary Jane	Del Shannon
Michelle	Beatles
Peggy Sue	Buddy Holly
Ramona	Bachelors
Rosanna	Toto
Rosie	Don Patridge
Sheila	Tammy Roe
Shirley	Shakin' Stevens
Susanna	Art Company
Sylvia	Focus

From the arrival of the first Beatles' album, Please Please Me, in May 1963 until January 1968, when Val Doonican climbed to the number one album spot with Val Doonican Rocks But Gently, only one non-rock album reached the top of the tables in the UK – and that was the soundtrack of the movie The Sound of Music. In 1966 it was the only album to spend the whole year in the best sellers lists. All in all, The Sound of Music soundtrack spent more weeks in the UK album charts than any other record.

For the whole of 1959 and a good part of 1960 the soundtrack of the movie South Pacific topped the best selling album charts in the UK. Although later albums were to outsell South Pacific in sheer volume, none has ever surpassed its duration at the top of the tables. In the USA a recording of South Pacific hit the number one spot for a record total of sixty-nine weeks, beginning in May 1949.

Frank Thoughts

'Most people wouldn't know music if it came up and bit them on the ass,' claimed Frank Zappa.

Facing up to the wave of rock 'n roll that threatened to sweep away the big band sound of the post-war years, American band leader Mitch Miller commented, 'It's not music, it's a disease.'

'I remember when I was very young, this is very serious, I read an article by Fats Domino which has really influenced me. He said, "You should never sing the lyrics out very clearly"' said Mick Jagger, which might explain a few things.

The world's greatest mouth-organist, Larry Adler, announced at a concert in New York that, due to typographical quirks in the local press, he was now known as 'a Leg-End in his own lifetime'!

> To the music of Rimsky-Korsakoff
> I could never take my corset off
> And where are the sailors who would pay
> To see me strip to Massenet?
>
> Gypsy Rose Lee

Bing Crosby

Bing Crosby was one of the most popular singers of the twentieth century. Dinah Shore gave her analysis of his success when she said: 'Bing Crosby sings like all people think they sing in the shower.'

When asked to compose his own epitaph, he decided upon, 'He was an average guy who could carry a tune.'

You don't have to be a great singer to have a number one hit record, as Rex Harrison, Telly Savalas and Lee Marvin have all proved. Harrison and Savalas wisely talked their way through 'On the Street Where You Live' and 'If', but Lee Marvin gave 'Wand'rin' Star' the full treatment – and reassured a lot of closet singers who had privately suspected that *they* had the worst voice in the world that they had nothing to be embarrassed about.

The Law Is an Ass

The year after Tommy Steele had climbed to the top of the British hit parade with 'Singing the Blues' and the year in which another six of his songs reached the charts, he made an appearance in court to give evidence in a case involving one of his contracts. The judge, reflecting his own familiarity with life outside his chambers, asked rhetorically at one point, 'How long can this Tommy Steele last? Five months?'

Three years later, on the first day of the 1960s, Tommy Steele rode to number six in the hit parade on the back of his 'Little White Bull', and he's still riding strong today.

Rock and roll is instant coffee.

Bob Geldof

Packing Up Your Troubles

The First World War, The Great War, wouldn't have been the same, as far as news-reels were concerned, without shots of the troops cheerfully marching past the cameras while choruses, or at the very least the melody, of 'Pack up your troubles in your old kit bags and smile, smile, smile' accompanied them to the front. The music for the song was written in 1915 by staff sergeant Felix Powell and won him first prize in a competition for the best morale-boosting song – a prize richly deserved.

Sergeant Powell didn't let this early success go to his head, all the same. In fact he let it go rather too far in the opposite direction. When the next war started Powell stuck it out for three years and then committed suicide.

Bitter Sweet

By far the severest musical bumps I've suffered have come from audience and critics. There was a time when I used to read bad notices and then carry them round in my inside pocket, to take them out in dark corners or secluded alleys to see if I could exorcise the effect by reading them again. This never worked and the reviews always brought immediate paralysis to the spirit and atrophy to the knees, reducing me to a state of near collapse.

There was one critic who dismissed me completely once, which is often the most hurtful form of criticism. He said he could take Peter Cook for maybe five minutes, but he couldn't take me at all! Curiously, several years later, he ate his words and decided that we were both wonderful. Perhaps I had got better, but I remained sceptical.

One bad review of *Thirty Is a Dangerous Age, Cynthia* came from a woman critic who asked her readers who I thought I was – some little sexpot? Eight years later, when Peter and I were in New York doing *Good Evening* she telephoned my hotel and suggested we had a drink! Is it that people think remarks like this get spirited away in some mildly alcoholic haze?

Now I try not to read notices and just ask friends to bear with me and only report unmitigated flattery – not that that works all the time. When we were first on Broadway with *Beyond the Fringe* Elaine May came backstage after one performance and told me, 'God, I loved the show.' 'Did you?' I foolishly asked. 'No,' she answered, seeing that she was in for five minutes of reassurance. So I actually don't know whether she liked it or not. I hope she did.

One of the first plays I was in at Oxford was a production of *Antony and Cleopatra*, directed by Anthony Page and for which I had written the music. We put this on at the little theatre in Abingdon a few miles away and I played Enobarbus. This was too much for an American friend of mine who sat in the third row one night and laughed out loud at me the entire time, even during my death scene when my most moving music should have been reducing him to tears.

Some time after the appearance of my film *10* a music

critic, reviewing a concert in which I'd played, wrote, 'I give him six out of ten as a pianist' and went on to criticize me for something that I had played entirely correctly. We'd been playing Beethoven's Triple Concerto, at the end of which are three bars that have just one short note at the beginning of each bar. However, there is a pedal mark all the way through, so you are supposed to keep the pedal down, with the effect that the piano sings through the gaps. The critic in question ticked me off for using the pedal too much, especially at the end! Forget about winning them all – sometimes it seems you can't win any, though at least, judging by what follows, I'm not alone in this.

Audience and Applause

'The custom of showing one's pleasure at beautiful music by immediately following it with an ugly noise' is how Percy Scholes defines applause in *The Oxford Companion to Music* (1955).

The subject is certainly a controversial one, but most artists would tend to disagree with him. Judy Garland, for example, is quoted as saying that 'Audiences have kept me alive', and her audiences were very far from silent. At the other end of the performing spectrum, Placido Domingo seems to agree with her. 'The one thing I hate about the Met', he says, 'is the note in the programme that the public is requested not to interrupt the music with applause.'

Some performers seem to demand applause almost as a right. In defending his refusal ever to play an encore, the pianist Artur Schnabel said that 'Applause is a receipt, not a bill.' He also said, 'I know two kinds of audience only – one coughing and one not coughing.'

Why do audiences applaud at all? The philosopher Jean-Jacques Rousseau had one theory: 'People applaud a prima-donna as they do the feats of the strong man at the fair. The sensations are painfully disagreeable, hard to endure, but one is so glad when it is all over that one cannot help rejoicing.'

In *The Importance of being Ernest*, by Oscar Wilde, Lady Bracknell has a very clear way of how audiences behave: 'If one plays good music people don't listen, and if one plays bad music people don't talk.'

Stravinsky was quite clear on the subject: 'I never understood the need for a "live" audience. My music, because of its extreme quietude, would be happiest with a dead one.'

One of the greatest jazz musicians of the twentieth century, Miles Davis, made his opinions equally plain. Of a lady who complained that she couldn't 'understand' a performance, he said: 'It took me twenty years' study and practice to work up to what I wanted to play in this performance. How can she expect to listen five minutes and understand it?'

Critical Analysis

In the days when George Bernard Shaw made his living as a music critic he found himself dining one evening in a restaurant where an orchestra entertained the clients with the popular music of the day. Recognizing Shaw, the conductor sent a message via his waiter asking whether Shaw would like to request something the orchestra might play. Shaw wrote one word on the card, 'Dominoes'.

'A critic,' said Whitney Balliet, 'is a bundle of biases held loosely together by a sense of taste,' while Alexandre Dumas pointed out that music is the only noise for which one is obliged to pay.

Caught with Your Baton Down

In the days when big dance bands were at the height of their popularity, their fans often had an uncanny ear to distinguish between the two hundred or so dance orchestras that serenaded American and European audiences. Among these, Mitchell Ayres, leader of one of the most popular American bands, discovered the consequences of underestimating his fans' perception. Finding himself double-booked one night, he left his band playing in their regular nightclub spot and travelled to a play at a school prom (for which he'd been booked months in advance), and brought in a few local players, in the hope that the kids wouldn't realize the substitution.

At least two of his audience were less than impressed, and taking a break in their car, turned on the radio to hear a welcome and familiar sound followed by the announcement that the network was now bringing them 'the music of Mitchell Ayres and his orchestra' from a restaurant in Tuckahoe, New York.

I was playing with the John Dankworth Band at a dance in Glasgow in about 1959 when a spot of bother flared up between two men on the dance floor. One had tried to cut in on a couple and in return for a tap on the shoulder the other guy landed a punch on him that sent him reeling across the floor. Others tried to come to the injured man's defence on his right to cut in, but each one of them was sent flying as well, the dancer hit them so hard. In between blows he kept on dancing apparently unperturbed and the band tried to keep on playing although we were all over the place and my fingers were trembling at the keyboard. That was one of the occupational hazards!

My advice to all who want to attend a lecture on music is 'Don't; go to a concert instead.'

Ralph Vaughan Williams

The critic Percy Hammond ended a scathing review of a soon-to-be-forgotten musical with the comment, 'I have knocked everything but the knees of the chorus girls, and nature has anticipated me there.'

At Home with Music

From the last century comes dismissive advice dished out by an author who preferred to be known by the self-effacing anonymity of 'A Member of the Aristocracy'. This worthy counselled would-be hostesses of musical gatherings:

> When music is given at afternoon 'at homes', it is usual to listen to the performance, or at least appear to do so; and if conversation is carried on, it should be done in a low tone, so as not to disturb or annoy the performers.

I actually like conversation going on during my performances which is why I enjoy playing in restaurants, though I also like the conversation to wind down as the music is gradually discovered.

Following an amateur concert in Wiltshire a hundred years ago the reporter from a local newspaper tactfully observed of a duet sung by two young ladies, 'It is a pity that the composer did not leave directions as to how flat he really did want it sung.'

More Beech – Amen!

Once, walking out into the auditorium to conduct a concert, the audience greeted Beecham with complete silence. He glared at it, then turned to the orchestra and said: 'Let us pray.'

I can share the sentiment. I soon gave up the idea of doing cabaret after I performed some of my musical parodies for an audience of medical students once. Musical parodies always went down terrifically well with the musical students but I'm the first to admit they might not have been quite a medical student's cup of tea. The evening had been a disaster as far as I was concerned and with one more piece to go I said as cheerfully as I could, 'I would now like to play...' at which one of the audience suggested, 'Now show us something funny.'

That would perhaps have been the most humiliating experience of my career had I not died on stage with Peter Cook at a Young Conservatives Ball we appeared at in London. We'd been in the habit of improvising stuff as Pete and Dud and duly took our seats on the stage. Peter has the alternately delightful and shocking habit of trying to embarass me, and in front of all these people he started going into the most obscene monologue which began, 'I was in the toilet the other day...' He spared no detail and he was greeted with dead silence. Relentlessly he carried on, searching for an exit line but for once in his life he couldn't find one. Eventually we ground to a halt and drifted offstage in absolute silence. I'd have to do something pretty dire to top that.

To know whether you are enjoying a piece of music or not, you must see whether you find yourself looking at the advertisements of Pears' soap at the end of the programme.

Samuel Butler

Hit from the Press

The press have been responsible for many unfortunate but unforgettable *doubles entendres*, usually by virtue of typographical error. One of the most famous came in a review of a concert, which stated that a famous soprano, '... ended her recital with a touching rendition of that charming Richard Rodgers ballad, "People will say we're in Hove."'

Other mistakes are made, however, by the writer. An advertisement in the magazine *The Strad* (a specialist magazine for string players) rather ambiguously stated that 'Our strings are used by a cross section of the Hallé orchestra.'

While the origins of many of these quotations are difficult to discover, one can be sure that several variations of the unintentional formula below have appeared over the years:

'John Pritchard conducts the LPO's second concert of the winter season at the White Rock Pavilion, Hastings, on Tuesday (7.30). The soloist will be Ronald Smith, who will play Tchaikovsky's Piano Concerto no. 1.

There will be another wrestling tournament at the Pavilion on Wednesday (7.45pm).'

Fritz Kreisler was walking once through New York with a friend, a conductor, when they passed a fish shop. Indicating the rows of glassy eyes and slack, open mouths on the marble slab, the conductor commented, 'That reminds me – I've got a concert tonight.'

The Critics

'They ply their saws, and timber and proud oaks are reduced to sawdust... Music sets nightingales to singing of love, but it sets pugdogs to yapping.' Thus Robert Schumann summed up his opinion of what Ralph Vaughan Williams called 'Misbegotten abortions' – the critics.

Hector Berlioz was characteristically lyrical about them as well. His comment on them was, 'Poor devils! Where do they come from? At what age are they sent to the slaughter house? What is done with their bones? Where do such animals pasture in the daytime? Do they have females, and young? How many of them have handled the brush before being reduced to the broom?'

This theme was carried through by another Frenchman, Erik Satie, who began a lecture in 1918 with the proposition, 'Last year, I gave several lectures on "Intelligence and Musicality in Animals". Today I shall speak to you about "Intelligence and Musicality in Critics". The subject is very similar.' Q.E.D.

Perhaps it is because of the power they wield, power that can literally make or break a career, that they are so universally disliked. Aaron Copland was succinct when he said that 'If a literary man puts together two words about music, one of them will be wrong.' Puccini thought that criticism was the most useless occupation in the world, adding, 'Critics love mediocrity.'

Of course, no one ever remembers when the critics were right, only when they made a mistake. George Moore hit the nail on the head in saying: 'The lot of critics is to be remembered by what they failed to understand.' Jean Sibelius struck a similarly gloomy note when he advised, 'Pay no attention to what the critics say: no statue has ever been put up to a critic.'

This was certainly advice followed by the famous pianist and showman Liberace. In response to critics who had all hated a concert he had given in 1954, he said: 'What you said hurt me very much. I cried all the way to the bank.' (Twenty years later he was to go further, by announcing, 'You remember that bank that I cried all the way to? I bought it!')

Characteristically, it was two jazz musicians who had the most sensible attitude to music criticism. Louis Armstrong insisted, 'There's only two ways to sum up music: either it's good or it's bad. If it's good you don't mess about with it; you just enjoy it.'

John Coltrane put it even more succinctly: 'If the music doesn't say it, how can words say it for the music?'

Honesty — The Best Policy?

Brahms was asked by a young composer if he could play the great man a funeral march he had written, dedicated to the memory of Beethoven. Brahms listened patiently while the young man played with all the artistry he could muster. When he had finished, Brahms said, 'I think that I would be much happier if Beethoven had written the march and *you* were dead.'

In another tale, Brahms is credited with more tact. The story goes that Max Bruch brought the score of his (now famous) first violin concerto to Brahms, and asked him to look at it. Brahms read the concerto from beginning to end, and hated it. He didn't wish to be rude to Bruch, however, and in an attempt to say something appreciative asked, 'Tell me, where *did* you get this manuscript paper?'

The first thing to do on arriving at a symphony concert is to express the wish that the orchestra will play Beethoven's Fifth. If your companion then says 'Fifth what?' you are safe for the rest of the evening.

Donald Ogden Stewart

> *A musicologist is someone who can read music but can't hear it.*
> *Sir Thomas Beecham*

Peter Ustinov

Peter Ustinov is a man whose views on music, as on many subjects, are either witty or astute, and frequently both. On the Soviet government's past policies on music and music-making, he said, 'Even if there is a subversive or reactionary way of playing Beethoven's Violin Concerto, it is frankly beyond the capabilities of the average commisar to detect it.'

In a more tongue-in-cheek mood, and perhaps betraying some of his own prejudices, he said about jazz, 'This is an art form which probably stems from a spirit of revenge by the negroes for having been taken to America at all.'

On producing opera: 'Opera singers learn to act quickly and soon master all the gestures. Unfortunately, they soon forget everything except the gestures. Not that it matters much, for on the first night they proceed to do exactly what they did in the last opera.' Perhaps because he is so accomplished in diverse fields, he holds that 'There is no incompatibility between Barnum and Beethoven; both have their place in a cultured society.' And he offered this pertinent comment on the inate snobbery of the English: 'Purcell, who died when Bach and Handel were ten years old, was a very great composer, whose importance in Britain would surely have been recognised earlier had his name been Heinrich Pürzel.'

> *Some musicians are not at all sure about what they compose. Ralph Vaughan Williams said, after hearing his 'London Symphony', 'I don't know whether I like it, but it is what I meant.' After some time, however, he revised his opinion and said: I realize now that it is not as boring as I thought it was.'*

Slings and Arrows

Of all composers, it seems that the one who has had to endure more insults than anyone else is Richard Wagner. Here is a selection of some of the more polite things his contemporaries said about him:

Wagner's music is better than it sounds.

Mark Twain

Wagner has beautiful moments, but dreadful quarter hours.

Gioacchino Antonio Rossini

Wagner, thank the fates, is no hypocrite. He says right out what he means, and he usually means something nasty.

James G. Huneker

Wagner is evidently mad.

Hector Berlioz

Is Wagner a human being at all? Is he not rather a disease?

Friedrich Nietzsche

I like Wagner's music better than any other music. It is so loud that one can talk the whole time without people hearing what one says. That is a great advantage.

Oscar Wilde

I love Wagner, but the music I prefer is that of a cat hung up by its tail outside a window and trying to stick to the panes of glass with its claws.

Charles Baudelaire

'*If Beethoven's Seventh Symphony is not by some means abridged, it will soon fall into disuse.*'
                        Boston music critic, Philip Hale, writing in 1837

Hair Today... Gone Tomorrow

Johann Strauss 'the younger' visited America in 1872 accompanied by his black-haired retriever of which he was inordinately fond. On their arrival the composer found his 'Blue Danube' waltz sweeping through the country and almost as popular as 'Yankee Doodle'.

Strauss was mobbed wherever he went, especially by women admirers, who took it into their heads to ask for a lock of hair from the composer's wavy black mane.

By the end of the tour hundreds of these gifts had been handed over, enough by rights to make Strauss bald. However, his head remained apparently unscathed and the source of the locks of dark hair remained a mystery until the day he left, again in the company of his dog that now looked more like a well clipped poodle!

Audience Participation

A year or two after the appearance of *The Jazz Singer*, its star, Al Jolson, found himself on stage in Memphis and playing to an audience that contained one persistent heckler. To silence the man Jolson called out to him, 'We should do a double-act. I'll sing "Swanee River" and you can jump in it.'

A music critic was overheard by the opera administrator Rudolf Bing saying, 'You know, George Szell is his own worst enemy.'
    '*Not while I'm still alive, he isn't!*', interjected Bing.

You Can Fool All of the People Some of the Time

In the case of the great Fritz Kreisler the fooling lasted for some considerable time.

The famous Austrian violinist was known to have interests in composition as well as playing. In 1919 Broadway was the setting for the first performance of his operetta *Apple Blossoms*, and he included among his other compositions a string quartet and some minor violin pieces. It seemed only natural, then, that he should be the man to unearth a number of lost musical treasures, which he started to include in his concerts. These included works like: W.F. Bach's 'Grave' for violin; Boccherini's Allegretto; Cartier's 'La Chasse'; Dittersdorf's Scherzo; Martini's Andantino; Porpora's Minuet; Tartini's Variations on a Theme by Corelli; and Vivaldi's Violin Concerto in C.

Many of these pieces became firm favourites with Kreisler's audiences. Some were even deemed to be 'little masterpieces' by the more enthusiastic. And music scholars must secretly have thanked Kreisler for saving them the trouble of combing through archives in months of laborious searching. No doubt Kreisler was delighted by the reception given to the 'Classical Manuscripts' as his discoveries were called – especially as he had composed all of them himself!

He broke the news calmly to an interviewer in the early part of 1935 and soon had a lot of eminent faces blushing with embarrassment. Not that the revelation really harmed Kreisler's professional reputation. As one American newspaper drily observed, all he had really done was to show that 'Business is, as the saying goes, business.'

Beethoven always sounds like the upsetting of bags – with here and there a dropped hammer.

John Ruskin

It Will Be All Right on the Night

The trials and tribulations suffered by even the most famous musicians make amusing reading, and for performers like myself they're a reminder that something goes wrong for almost everyone.

Take the debut performance of Pablo Casals, the great cellist. He was so nervous that his bow hand seized up completely and he had to give it a good shake to loosen his grip – how I sympathize. The next thing he knew, the bow had gone sailing into the audience, who dutifully returned it to him, passing it carefully from row to row.

Even more alarming was the experience of Beethoven, who once gave a performance of a new piano concerto in which he forgot that he was the piano soloist and not the conductor. At one point in the proceedings he began to conduct the orchestra so vigorously that his outflung arms knocked over the candles that were lighting his music and the performance ground to a halt. Two boys were recruited to hold the lights when the concerto restarted, but the composer forgot himself again, and knocked the candle out of one boy's hand. The other saw what was coming and ducked, and the audience, enjoying this unexpected interlude, made the mistake of laughing. This infuriated Beethoven so much that he hit the keyboard with his fist – and broke six piano strings!

But even Beethoven would never haved faced the kind of problem that Boy George experienced when he flew into Nice Airport and was refused entry into France on the grounds that though his passport described him as male, his long hair, earrings and make-up were those of a woman. For three hours the Culture Club star argued that, despite appearances, he was a man, until finally the British Consulate had to be called in to verify his sex. At this the airport officials gave way, excusing their action by saying that French immigration laws do not permit transvestites to enter the country...

The Lost Chords

Webern's music is notoriously difficult to understand. It is 'modern music' at its most complicated, and until very recently was largely unknown.

The story is told of one music critic who was supposed to review a concert of Webern's music, a rare event that was on for only one night. His consternation when he missed the train was therefore understandable. What was he going to do? For once in his career he decided to cheat, and the next morning bought the only recording of this particular piece.

He listened to it several times at home, before beginning to write. The end of the piece he found particularly interesting: the instruments all played a final chord which began at the very top of the scale, and slowly all got lower and lower, and eventually just stopped.

The critic thought that this was a marvellous device, and wrote a vivid description of the piece, in the guise of the previous night's concert, which said that its end had:

a deep significance, an importance far greater than the piece itself. The final chord begins as a fierce, piercing shriek, which is almost as if music itself is crying for help. The chord slides lower down the scale, until the lowest notes possible on each instrument are reached. It is almost as if this were symbolic of the problem of modern music – searching for somewhere new to go, but simply descending lower into the depths, confused and without direction.

The review duly appeared, and caused quite a stir. Had the reviewer heard the same piece as everyone else? Certainly, no one recognized his description of the ending!

So it was with a rather red face that the reviewer found out why his deceit had back-fired and caused such controversy – his record-player had an auto-stop which had cut the record off thirty seconds before the end, and the descending chord was simply the turntable slowing down and stopping!

Chopin Changing

Most musicians manage to establish a reasonable harmony with music critics, though there a few who find it impossible to coexist with them; which usually brands them as critic-haters for the whole of their professional lives. One such was the virtuoso pianist, Vladimir Pachmann, who, in addition to his widely known views about critics, was also acknowledged to be one of the greatest interpreters of Chopin's music. This led to probably his greatest personal antagonism, with a Berlin critic who regarded himself as an authority on Chopin.

At one of his concerts in that city, Pachmann decided to show up the man for what he thought him to be – a sycophantic fraud. So when he appeared on the stage the audience was interested to see the great pianist proudly bearing a pair of socks – the very pair, he announced, that George Sand had knitted for Chopin himself. That said, he laid the socks reverently on the piano where they remained to lend inspiration to his playing.

The following morning Pachmann stayed in his rooms expecting a caller and, as he'd hoped, the despised critic duly arrived, to ask whether he might be allowed a glimpse of the Chopin socks; perhaps he might even handle them.

Pachmann said he was happy to oblige so esteemed a colleague and presented the man with the socks, which he raised to his lips, and kissed in adoration.

An embarrassingly short time after his departure rumours began spreading among Berlin's musical society that some 'misunderstanding' had taken place over the socks. Pachmann had apparently informed close friends that the pair he had offered to the critic were really a well-worn pair of his own which had somehow become separated from his washing and had been hanging round for a fortnight!

The attraction of the virtuoso for the public is very like that of the circus for the crowd. There is always the hope that something dangerous will happen.

Debussy

Critical Quotes

I don't like my music, but what is my opinion against that of millions of others?

Frederick Loewe

Critics can't even make music by rubbing their back legs together.

Mel Brooks

Of the audience at a chamber-music concert, an Oxford don once remarked, 'They look like the sort of people who go to the English Church abroad.'

W.H. Auden

Classical music: the kind we keep hoping will turn into a tune.

Kin Hubbard

So Musical a Discord

For the majority of concert-going audiences avant-garde music is still something of an acquired taste. Sixty years ago it proved an even greater challenge and composers set on exploring new musical frontiers had to be prepared for mixed responses.

Among the early pioneers in this field was the American composer George Antheil, who counted among his works the 'Ballet mécanique', which he scored for an enterprising range of instruments that included a fire siren, aeroplane propellers, car horns, sixteen player-pianos, anvils, two octaves of electric bells and assorted pieces of tin and steel. The sound produced by this ensemble had a variety of effects on its audiences, though none more visibly dramatic than that of a man who heard the piece during a concert at Carnegie Hall. As a gesture of defeat, he attached his handkerchief to his walking stick, while the 'Ballet mécanique' was still in progress, and waved this above his head to signal his surrender.

You Don't Say!!!

In analysing one familiar piece of music, Professor Wilfred Mellers of York University observed, 'It is quintessential. It exists in the moment, without before or after. For although the key signature is the E flat beloved of Tin Pan Alley, the opening phrase is pentatonic, or perhaps an Aeolian C which veers towards E flat. The timeless, present-affirming modality is instinctive...'

Was he talking about a work of Stravinsky's perhaps, or a Beethoven quartet? No, the subject of this learned exegesis was The Beatles' hit 'She Loves You'. Yeah, Yeah, Yeah...

Hiss Off

When Igor Stravinsky's score for the ballet the *Rite of Spring* was first heard in Paris its strange dissonances and unusual rhythms so outraged the conservative tastes of the audience that they started hissing in protest. Before long there was a complete uproar, through which the lone voice of the ballet's promoter could be heard imploring, 'First listen! Then boo!'

Thirty-nine years later, when the *Rite of Spring* was again performed in Paris, it was greeted with tremendous applause. The conductor, who had also directed the orchestra on the first occasion, commented afterwards, 'There was just as much noise as the last time, but the tonality was different.'

Beware Lehrer, Stilgoe, Flanders, Swann, et al

If any person has sung or composed against another person a song such as was causing slander or insult to another, he shall be clubbed to death.

Roman Law, Twelve Tables, 449 BC

Rear Attacks

The German composer Max Reger achieved sweet revenge on a music critic with this reply to his notice: 'I am sitting in the smallest room in the house. I have your review in front of me. Soon it will be behind me.'

Commenting on a musical he had recently seen, Kenneth Tynan noted, 'It contains a number of those tunes one goes into the theatre humming.'

Seventh Heaven

Among the eight records I selected as my *Desert Island Discs* for Roy Plomley there were four fairly heavy black-cassocked pieces: Kathleen Ferrier (who has one of my favourite voices) singing from Mahler's 'Songs on the Death of Children', something written by Thomas Tomkins about Abraham on the point of giving Isaac the chop and weeping a lot, a passage from the Mozart *Requiem* and then the great B minor organ fugue by Bach, which has a wonderfully deep lugubriousness about it.

I've always loved that richness that comes from music that has a contemplation of the grave, so it seems only right to conclude this eclectic wander through the by-ways of music with some thoughts on the great hereafter.

Don't be perturbed – they're brief, but I hope interesting in shedding a little light on how a few of music's famous names passed from this world to the next.

Death, Where Is Thy Sting?

If you happen to meet the Austrian composer Alban Berg in the great hereafter, put that question to him and he'll tell you in no uncertain terms. Poor Berg died of blood poisoning brought on initially by an insect bite in the small of his back.

He was just one of a number of distinguished composers who have shuffled off their mortal coil in a variety of unusual ways. Some have died in the pursuit of their art; one such was Jean Baptiste Lully, court musician to Louis XIV. After being commissioned to compose a Te Deum in celebration of his royal master's recovery from a serious illness, he mounted the podium to give the new work its first performance and by a sad irony began to conduct what turned out to be his own requiem. In those days it was standard for the conductor to beat time with a stick, in Lully's case a large, heavy walking stick. As his excitement mounted during the Te Deum, his concentration wavered and in a burst of enthusiasm he brought the stick crashing

down on his big toe. This led immediately to painful
swelling which became a very unpleasant abscess in a
couple of days. The court physician was called for and
advised the immediate amputation of the toe, followed
only a short time later by the foot and finally Lully's whole
leg, though by this stage even this drastic measure wasn't
enough to spare his life, and from that one rash blow the
poor man went to meet his Maker.

Charles Henry Valentin Alkan was another French
musician who could be said to have died for his art. This
nineteenth-century piano virtuoso, whose own compositions advanced the technical resources of piano composition, lived a secluded life dedicated to music and it was in
that manner that he died – reaching to the top of a bookcase
and accidentally pulling the whole piece of furniture and its
contents down on top of him.

At the end of the Second World War Anton Webern was
tragically shot by an American sentry who mistook him for
a terrorist out after the curfew.

A similar fate awaited Michael Wise, the seventeenth-
century organist and master of the choristers at St Paul's
Cathedral. He died following a violent quarrel with his
wife, as a result of which he dashed into the street and
started raining blows on the first person he set eyes on.
Unfortunately for Wise this turned out to be one of the
nightwatchmen, who traded blows with Wise. The
watchman, armed with a club, came off the better and St
Paul's lost its organist to a badly fractured skull.

Bad luck quite literally dogged the American composer
Wallingford Riegger, who met his end when he tripped
over the leads of two dogs milling round his feet, banged
his head and slipped into the next world in spite of
emergency brain surgery.

Then there are those musicians who have been more or
less architects of their own destiny. Tchaikovsky was one
of these. Four days after the unfavourable reception with
which his Pathetic Symphony had been received in St
Petersburg the great composer, despondent some said,
already feeling ill according to others, deliberately drank a
glass of unboiled water in the middle of a cholera epidemic.

His friends who witnessed this were appalled, though Tchaikovsky told them that he was less afraid of cholera than other illnesses. Cholera, however, did not share his opinion and it soon finished him off.

Standard reference books state in sober terms that Janacek died in the arms of his mistress. You have to turn to less discreet volumes to discover that part of the reason for this was that the lady happened to be in bed with the seventy-four-year-old composer when he pushed himself just a little too far and succumbed to a heart attack.

It was the pursuit of physical pleasure that finished off the Prague-born composer Franz Kotzwara in 1793. He had developed a taste for exotic, some would say decidedly kinky, ways of being turned on, most of which involved elaborate methods of bondage. On the night of his death he persuaded a London prostitute to tie him up in such a way that he was suspended from the ceiling completely helpless. Under normal circumstances Kotzwara arranged to be cut down after five minutes. However, on the night in question his 'companion' was quite unable to revive him. She was tried for murder, but acquitted when the full circumstances were presented to the jury.

Famous Last Words

Beethoven
'I shall hear in Heaven.'
(The most poignant of them all.)

Brahms – after finishing a glass of wine
'Ah, that tastes nice, thank you.'

Hans Guido von Bülow – asked how he was feeling
'Bad.'

Enrico Caruso
'Doro, I can't get my breath!'

Kathleen Ferrier
'Now I'll have eine kleine pause...'

Grieg
'Well, if it must be so...'
(And it was)

Haydn
'Cheer up, children, I'm all right.'
(Wrong this time, though.)

Al Jolson
'This is it. I'm going, I'm going.'

Lehar
'Now I have finished with all earthly business, and high time too. Yes, yes, my dear child, now comes death.'

Liszt
'Tristan!'

Mahler
'Mozart!'

Mendelssohn – asked how he was feeling
'Tired, very tired.'

Moussorgsky
'It is the end. Woe is me!'

Mozart – referring to the score of the *Requiem* on which he was working
'Did I not tell you that I was writing this for myself?'

Ravel – seeing his bandaged head in a mirror
'I look like a Moor.'

Schubert – on being told that he was lying in his own bed
'No! It's not true; Beethoven is not laid here.'
'Here, here is my end.'

Strauss – advised to get some sleep
'I will whatever happens.'

Wagner
'I am fond of them, of the inferior beings of the abyss, of those who are full of longing.'

Endpiece

Obituaries written about great artists are frequently embarrassing, and often too gushing in their praise. One of the most simple, and hence most powerful posthumous tributes must be what John O'Hara wrote when George Gershwin died of a brain tumour at the age of thirty-nine. He said: 'George Gershwin is dead, but I don't have to believe it if I don't want to.'